This book is dedicated to Dr. Galen Lueking.

A gentle giant among physicians; a fierce warrior for the underdog; the best friend our community has ever had; and the last of the mule-riding, suspenders-wearing country doctors. I never believed anyone to be irreplaceable, until now. And yes, I promise to accompany you on your next trail ride and serve as your beer wench. Happy trails, Doc.

Mascot Books
560 Herndon Parkway #120
Herndon, VA 20170
info@mascotbooks.com

Library of Congress Control Number: 2014941738

PRBVG0714A

ISBN-13: 9781620866702

Printed in the United States

www.mascotbooks.com

Movin' On

Memoirs of a Traveling Country Nurse

Barbara Fout Tackitt

illustrated by

Denise Plumlee-Tadlock

MASCOT® BOOKS

A Note to the Reader

The title of this book is dual-purposed. First, it represents me professionally, indicating my journey as I travel down the rural, country roads on my day-to-day route, moving from one patient's home to another. Secondly, it refers to my all of my wonderful patients who once walked upon our Earth but have now died and moved on spiritually. And lastly, Movin' On refers to me personally. With great anticipation, I try to eagerly "move on" to the next chapter of my life each time a new one begins. Hopefully retirement will be everything I have dreamed of it being, and with the best spouse in the world by my side, how can it not?

Introduction

For the past thirty years, I've made my living by traveling the small, rural Illinois county roads providing medical care to its most frail and elderly residents. I am a home health nurse. I go to the homes of the very ill and those confined to teach them how to medically care for themselves. My primary job was to educate them and give them necessary tools to make better choices. Some of them had frightening, intense needs such as complicated wound care, IV's, catheters, or Insulin injections. The goal was for them become independent enough to master their own diseases. But something very ironic happened along the way.

The patients I am going to write about, one in each chapter, are real. They all unknowingly did something that shaped who I am as a nurse, wife, mother, daughter, and overall person. Without intending, they taught me something. They had no clue they were teachers and educators too, but they were. I thank each and every one of them for being part of my life, both professionally and personally. I like to think that I am a better person for having known them.

Prologue

When I was eighteen I wondered, What in the world am I going to do with my life? I was graduating from high school and had absolutely no direction. To make matters worse, I was a last minute transplant to St Clair, Michigan, moving during my senior year after living in the same small town in southern Illinois my entire life.

My mom, a divorcee trying to raise four children alone, had met a wonderful man from Michigan and asked if I would be willing to move if she married him. She realized what she was asking, and was agreeable to put her life on hold and let me finish school if that's what I wanted. But true to my predictable, forecasted nature as the middle child with three brothers, I was eager to please. I wanted my Mom to be happy and chose her happiness over finishing my last year of high school where my roots were deeply planted. After all, I was a cheerleader, class officer, and as they say, my "dance card" was continually full. I thought the world revolved around me.

In spite of my desire to graduate in Cisne, Illinois, the call to move was stronger. So I left my forty lifetime classmates and moved to a school with an unimaginable 1,200 students. Needless to say, I was lost and remained lost for the rest of my time in St. Clair. Understand that there is nothing wrong with St. Clair. My surroundings were just very foreign and they came with unusually bad timing. I had lived on a farm with cows and chickens and was now living in a large northern city with things like snowmobiles and ice skates. I desperately missed my friends and my former life.

As my senior year was drawing to a close, a letter came to me from a classmate in Illinois, Linda Taylor. She stated that she wanted to be a nurse, and had been accepted to the Decatur Memorial Hospital (DMH) School of Nursing and was thrilled. Hmmm, I thought, a nurse. Even though I had no prior desire to become one, I thought the nursing uniforms were cute and at least it would be something to do.

I quickly wrote Linda back and asked about the application process. Remember, this was 1973 and there was no such thing as Google. Within a few weeks I had obtained the necessary paperwork from DMH and quickly sent it away. Time was a factor as graduation was already upon us. I had to travel to Decatur for a face to face interview and left discouraged. With my less than enthusiastic attitude, and most likely inappropriate answers to the deluge of questions, I was sure I made quite an impression; but at least I tried. As it were, there were only seventy-five students selected out of 300 applicants, and I happened to be one of the lucky ones. I had a suspicion that I was accepted because of some affirmative action thing or being required to accept a certain percentage of out of state students. But then again, maybe it didn't. At any rate, I was in and the stage was set. Linda and I spent the next three years developing a tremendous nursing knowledge base that has supported me throughout my career.

My first job as a registered nurse was in our small twenty-bed hospital in Flora, Illinois. I was the second-shift supervisor and often the only registered nurse (RN) in the hospital. At about 5:00 PM, after the day-people had all gone home, I became a one woman show. The Emergency Room bell would ring and I would have to leave my medical/surgical patients and tend to whatever surprise awaited me around the corner. The nature of the ER call could be anything from a feverish child or a car accident victim to crushing chest pain or an assortment of many other things.

If someone in the ER was admitted, I went to the front office with them, unlocked the door, and turned on the lights. We sat down at the typewriter and filled out the admission data sheet. They were then escorted to their room in a wheelchair. Once they were settled in, I unlocked the pharmacy and filled their medications, opened the cafeteria and fixed them a supper tray, and then did a number of other things that were required to make the patient safe and comfortable.

The problem was, there were many nights I never made it back to my medical/surgical patients and that bothered me a lot. Some were fresh surgical patients that were never checked, critical heart attack patients unattended except by the aide, there were IVs that ran dry, and meds that were passed late. In those days, that's just how it was. There was no round-the-clock doctor or ancillary staff. I finally couldn't take it. Even though I was young and inexperienced, I knew it wasn't right. Medical ligations were not as common as they are now, but they were still present and a fact of life. It was only a matter of time until I made a critical error. Since I had no way to change the system, I felt forced to leave. I loved my job, but my conscience told me I needed to move on.

The next eight years were spent safely in the confines of a doctor's office. I was happy there but after a few years, I felt all I was doing was carrying a cup of urine up and down the hall. My career went from having unlimited autonomy and independence at the hospital, to always having a physician right by my side. I no longer had to think or use any judgment. I felt unchallenged, as if I was wasting my professional career. The bulk of my daily conversations went something like this:

"How are you?"

"Great. Great. Isn't the weather beautiful/terrible today?"

"How are the kids?"

"Great. Nice to see you."

"I'll take your pee. The doctor will be in shortly."

Professionally, things had to change drastically and they had to change quickly. Surely my skills were being wasted and better things waited.

That fall I saw a "position opening" in our local newspaper. A home health nurse was needed for the Clay County Health Department. I wasn't exactly sure what that was. I thought they just went door to door and checked blood pressures. But I figured, whatever they did, it had to be better than the rut I was in. The Health Department Administrator called the day he received my application and I was hired on the spot. In retrospect, that should have raised some red flags. At the time I had no idea what I had gotten myself into.

My first day working for the Clay County Health Department was November 18, 1985. The sunrise brought with it a blizzard of epic ferocity. While driving forty miles-per-hour to my first client's house I thought, What have I gotten myself into? Where is the doctor? Where is my warm office? My shoes were soaked, my feet were freezing, my car was sliding all over the road, and I was behind schedule, but something surprising happened. I felt myself feeling liberated and joyful for the first time in years. I remember thinking, I could learn to enjoy this newfound challenge. And enjoy it I did.

What I'm about to share with you is a thirty-year collection of some of the most interesting people I've ever met in my life. They are not diplomats, celebrities, politicians, or fabulously wealthy. They are the ordinary people of rural Illinois, each with an extraordinary gift. Every chapter contains an actual patient with a real encounter. What started out as routine home visits, turned into lessons that remained with me for the rest of my life.

** *When possible, I attached actual photo's to authenticate the story. Unfortunately, after nearly 30 years, many of the subjects and their homes have long gone. In that case, I substituted the photo with an illustration.*

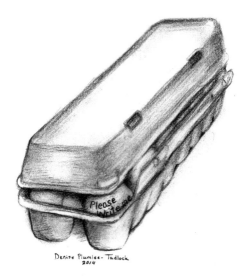

Denise Plumlee-Tadlock
2014

Pearl

When I first met Pearl, she was quiet, shy, and reserved; almost stoic. Tall and slender, she had perfect posture. She spoke with calculated correctness and appeared to have little interest in what I had to say. When being examined, she answered the questions appropriately but she was all business like Joe Friday on Dragnet. "Just the facts, Ma'am." She had no outside interests. Her curiosity was not piqued by either the local or national news. Our conversations were very professional and businesslike until the day Pearl trusted me enough to share her life, her past. I asked how long she had been married. That's all it took. To my amazement, her face lit up and she said it was "sixty years this year". She was very proud of her marriage and her husband, Ted. With the rate of unsuccessful marriages now days, why wouldn't she be? She said with a gleam in her eye, "Would you like to know how I met my husband?" With that, a most interesting story unfolded.

Pearl was born in 1908, living through good times and many

hardships. She lived during horse and buggy days, the depression, and WWII. As a young woman, Pearl went to work for Winston-Salem College in North Carolina. This was just prior to the attack on Pearl Harbor. She worked in the kitchen at the college preparing the meals for those fortunate enough to attend. One morning she opened a carton of eggs for the faculty breakfast and encountered something strange. An egg in the crate had a hand written message. It contained the name and address of a young soldier located in Flora, Illinois. The message simply said, "Please write me."

Well, Pearl was in quite a quandary as she felt very drawn to write this young man, this "Ted Upton". But, as she relayed to me, "I didn't know what to do. I already had a fella." Something spoke to her heart and she did indeed go straight home and respond to the egg request.

Ted was enlisted in the United States Army and while home on leave he wrote the note. He had the opportunity to do it because during his short leave from the military in Flora, he went to work at Brown's Poultry House. Brown's Poultry House processed chickens for retailing. Pete Bearead's job was to wring the chicken's neck, dip them in hot water, and then pluck the feathers. Pete and Ted worked together to gather any eggs that had been laid by the unknowing chickens. The eggs were then placed on a special light that looked much like a tin can. The light allowed the workers to see through the eggs. This process would be the equivalent of today's quality assurance programs. The eggs were found to be in one of three categories: rotten, with chick, or approved for sale. The first two were destroyed but the approved eggs were placed on a carton and prepared for shipment. The front of the store sold the eggs to customers, but all you had to do was look over the shoulder of cashier to see the whole process.

Redtop West was just a young boy when Ted worked at the

Poultry House. He and his large family lived just two houses down from the building. This was a rather odd arrangement as it meant the chicken processing plant was situated right in the middle of town. I'm not sure which came first, the business or the homes. (I will refrain from saying "the chicken or the egg".) Today's city ordinances would never permit such a pairing. In addition to the chicken processing procedure, Redtop also re-members a strong foul smell coming from the building. As a side business, the Browns also took in cow skins, or rawhides, and dried them in the basement. The aroma from the tanning could be "enjoyed" for blocks.

Redtop purged his guilt to me as he relayed the following sto-ry. When he was a young boy, his house always had a yard full of kids. Some belonged to his mother and father, some were friends of numerous siblings, and some were neighborhood kids. Grow-ing up poor may have one advantage. It can make a person pretty creative in getting money to purchase the desired goody: Baby Ruth candy bars, Sugar Daddies, Topps baseball trading cards which included a single stick of gum, or a nice cold Coca-Cola in a glass bottle. None of those things would come without mon-ey, so what was a guy to do? At night, Redtop and some of his clan would sneak over to Browns Poultry House and let the chickens out. The next day, as "good boys" should, they rushed over to the Poultry House to help when they saw the Browns frantically trying to gather up the chickens. The Browns were al-ways very grateful to those nice young men who sacrificed their morning ritual of bike riding and ball playing. As a reward, they paid each boy five cents for every chicken they caught. Redtop saw it as a win-win. The Brown's got their chickens back, he got some coins for his pocket.

Redtop also remembered that for years Mrs. Brown would bring his mother free eggs leftover from the day. Apparently it was Mr. Brown who obtained the strict business sense in the family-run business, because it was also Mrs. Brown who would sneak the West family chicken pieces under the eggs. She knew how poor they were and that they could use the extra food. But back to poor, undecided Pearl. Soon after sending that first letter, they found themselves corresponding regularly. Ted wrote and asked if he purchased a train ticket, would she be willing to come to Illinois to meet him. He still worked at the Poultry House which was located just a couple blocks from the train depot. With some trepidation she agreed. Pearl arrived in Flora, and within three weeks they were married. It still amazes me to think, at the time she was telling me the story they had just celebrated sixty years together.

One evening after they had been married several months, Ted was called back to the military. He was on his way to Chicago to report for duty when his Model A got a flat tire, which was not uncommon back then. Ted pulled to the side of the road to change the tire. That's when a truck came along and hit him, then drove off. The force of the impact threw him into the rain-filled ditch. He laid there until the next morning and it was light enough to see him. A man passing by saw Ted in the ditch and at first thought Ted was dead. When he realized the broken man was still breathing he picked him up, threw him in the back seat, and drove him Cook County Hospital. Ted remained in a coma for several weeks. Perhaps it was the sound of Pearl's voice that pulled him out of it, telling him to be strong because they had their first child on the way. Ted did remain strong, and was eventually transferred to Flora to rehabilitate in a nursing home, then he returned home. Ten months after their son was born, a daughter followed. Go, Ted!

What I Learned

With each piece of information that I learned from

Pearl and her family I said, "Oh my goodness!" Once she opened up, I found her remarkable. But what impressed me the most about her story was how different everything is for us today. We make our lives, or choices, so unnecessarily hard. Today, in search of our life-long soul mate, we have Match.com and eHarmony. Finding the "perfect" mate is as easy as checking boxes, analyzing data, and then being presented over the internet to the person of your dreams. I don't know what the success rate is for long-term relationships after being mathematically and scientifically calculated with today's questionnaires, but I doubt it rivals Pearl's. Sometimes in this life, you just have to take a leap of faith.

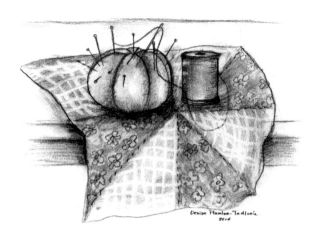

Bessie

Although many of my stories revolve around rural country folk, Bessie lived right on the edge of town. She lived alone and had been in failing health for many years. In this particular summer, she suffered a stroke which compromised her ability to continue to stay at home and care for herself. The nurse's visits helped, but that still left 23 hours in the day for her to be self-sufficient. Cooking, laundry, shopping, and all of the activities of daily living were becoming too much for her. Arrangements were being made for her to sell her home and move in with her daughter in another state. Although she knew it was necessary, she was still sad about leaving her home.

On one of my last visits with her, something jumped out and caught my eye. In her back yard, she had several quilts hanging on the clothesline. Being a quilt collector and enthusiast, I was naturally drawn to them. There were three hand-pieced, hand-quilted quilts and two hand-pieced tops. For those of you who may not know much about quilting, anytime either just the top or the entire quilt is hand crafted, the value is ten times one that has been done by machine. They were especially nice as the pieces were very small, making the detail even more intricate. The quilts could have easily been worth $750.

Upon questioning, Bessie did confirm that she had made the quilts, all by hand. I told her how much I loved quilts and admired anyone who had the patience and talent for such small detail. She wondered if I would like to have a bit of history on them and proceeded to tell me. They were true "scrap quilts" being put together with left over fabric, or scraps, from a prior project. She used to sew for her family and had an abundance of colors and patterns.

I also wondered why they were hanging on the clothes line. She said that she was airing them out because she was moving and she was trying to organize her things. Since she knew I had an interest in quilts, she asked if I would be interested in purchasing them. I said, "Sure, how much do you want for them?"

Now remember, a hand-pieced, hand-quilted quilt can run several hundred dollars. It is a dying craft and few people alive today have truly mastered the art. She thought for a moment then said, "If you will take all five of them, I will let you have them for $20." Twenty dollars! I told Bessie I would love to have them but that wasn't enough and she should ask for more. She stated that she no longer cared for the quilts and would be happy to see me have them. Not caring for or no longer wanting the quilts did not de-value them, at least as far as market value.

I went straight back to my office and called the daughter where Bessie was moving. I wanted her daughter to realize what her mother was doing. That she was selling cherished keepsakes for pennies on the dollar. I was afraid Bessie's stroke had left her with impaired mental capabilities. Her daughter said, and I recall it like it was yesterday, "I don't want those things either. If you want them for $20, then please take them."

Not being satisfied with that answer, I went to my administrator's office and told him the story. He felt I had covered all the bases and said if the patient, who was her own power of attorney, and her daughter were okay with it. I had his blessing. Needless to say, my tires nearly squealed leaving the parking lot. I still have them today, every one of them. I did proceed with having the two tops hand quilted and still keep them with the others.

What I Learned

It is difficult to put into words what I learned from this patient. As far as policy and procedure were concerned, I did what was right. I never felt as though I took advantage of the patient, or my position in the community. If I didn't acquire those quilts for $20, somebody else would have. I checked with her family and my boss. However, even given that, there is still a nagging sense of wrongdoing that has been eating away at me for thirty years. In my heart of hearts I felt I had done something unethical.

Someone once told me that when in a situation where I didn't know if it was proper, ask yourself, "Does it pass the smell test?" And this didn't. It didn't then and it doesn't now. On paper everything was proper. But in my heart, I felt like I had stolen those quilts. It did not pass the smell test. Period. Never again did I engage in flea marketing on the side of home care.

The Ridge

One beautiful, summer afternoon after I had completed my round of nursing visits, the need arose for someone to take medication to a patient in Tick Ridge. My husband had just presented me with a beautiful, bright-red convertible Mustang, so I was naturally the first person to volunteer to get out in the warm summer breeze and enjoy my new toy. After all, I was only thinking of the patient!

My convertible was a thing of beauty. Although the car was a 1994 model and 12 years old, it only had 14,000 miles and was otherwise flawless. Having been garage-kept all of its life, the paint was unscratched and the shine on it was magnificent. Special chrome rims sparkled and shone, which allowed the wheels to stand at attention. The initial car owner had a Flowmaster Exhaust system installed right after driving it off the showroom floor. At the turn of the key, the engine roared with that familiar low rumble that turned heads for blocks away. The CD player was usually blasting Frankie Valley and the Four Seasons. "Big girls don't cry, they don't cry-yi-yi, they don't cry!" Boom! Boom!

Boom! The loud muffler and the pulsating 60s music made me feel…well…alive! Rich, spoiled, pampered, and cool!

Don't get me wrong. I worked hard, as did my husband, and we both appreciated everything we got. Nothing we possessed was ever handed to us on a silver platter, so maybe that's why this Mustang was special. We even had vanity plates made for it that said "YeeHaw".

As I headed to Tick Ridge that afternoon, I had the top down, music blaring, sunglasses on, and my blonde hair blowing in the wind. Life was good. That was before I turned off the highway heading to The Ridge.

It is somewhat difficult to describe Tick Ridge. If you were to look for it on a map or Google it, you would come up empty-handed. Much the way the Tackitts are known by our Hangin' Rock location, the same holds true for the residents of Tick Ridge. Hangin' Rock and Tick Ridge are locations known only to locals, and these family heritages often define who we are.

"Where you folks from?" someone would ask.

"Hangin' Rock."

"Ooooh," they would say. "Them's good people."

Many of the residents of Tick Ridge are related. This is obvious by the rows of mailbox names that line the road: Tom Smith, Bill Smith, Sam Smith, Harold Smith, and so on. These are good people too. They take care of themselves and each other. Rarely is the law ever dispatched to Tick Ridge. Rumor has it that Big Earl takes care of disputes within the Ridge. Being born and raised in the Ridge, Big Earl is a family elder and is often regarded as the quintessential Godfather, looking out for and protecting his turf. I don't know if this is true or not, but somehow they never need official law enforcement assistance with their problems. They seem to take care of their own matters. Honestly, I think Big Earl does exist, and he keeps a tight rein on his territory.

The poverty level there is overwhelming. As I was driving to my patient, I noticed how close the trailers and houses were to the road. Many of the houses were without grass or operating cars. Large dogs lurched from chains that had worn a bald circle around dead trees. Each home seemed to have a scattering of small and dirty-faced children.

One particular trailer had a garden hose running from an outside spigot up through the kitchen window, no doubt needed to wash dishes and flush the toilet. No running water was available for the trailer so this solution was the next best thing. As I drove slowly along I noticed that most of the adults were home, in spite of it being mid-day. I recall that the people in their yards stopped what they were doing and walked to the edge of the road to watch the "rich lady in the fancy car", or at least that's how I felt. I'd never felt so self-conscious, out of place, or humbled in my life. Instead of showing them my sincere concern and demonstrating my ability to connect and relate to them, I did just the opposite. I sank lower and lower in my seat, kept driving, and simply disappeared as I drove out of sight. I never stopped, nor went back. I was embarrassed and ashamed of my lack of sensitivity. I asked another nurse to deliver the medication the next day.

What I Learned

The first question I had to ask myself in regards to the Tick Ridge experience was this: When did I get put in charge of being so awesome? I've always heard that when you give a speech, you should know your audience. The same holds true for home visits, especially if you're tooling around in a sporty car. The Bible says "Pride cometh before the fall." In other words, if you are too full of yourself, something usually happens along the way to show that you are not quite as awesome as you think you are. I certainly lacked good judgment by driving my new, little convertible sports car in an area where the residents lacked even the most basic life-sustaining necessities. What was I thinking? I never viewed my car the same. I still drove it and still loved it, but was careful to think before driving it to a patient's home.

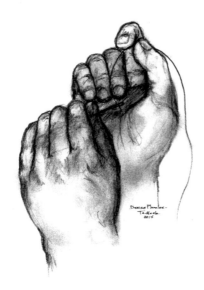

Noah

Rotund, stocky, and portly are some of the adjectives I'd use to describe Noah. He was a large man with beautiful white hair. He was nearly as round as he was tall and had huge bear-claw like hands. Years of hard work had left him in declining health, which was where I came in. I treated the large hole in his ankle, created by poor circulation. He did very little cooking for himself and even less house-cleaning or personal care. He simply couldn't. Noah's vision was poor and arthritis had made simple tasks like tying shoes nearly impossible. Noah was a very likable character and, not surprisingly, he was proud of his career and his retirement.

By trade, he was a B&O Railroad worker. He was the foreman for a crew of track workers that was called a Section Gang. Until fairly recent times, the jobs of laying track or maintaining railroad roadbeds was the responsibility of Section Gangs who performed the work by sheer physical labor.

Another common name for such laborers was Gandy Dancer,

derived from their use of tools made by the Gandy Manufacturing Company of Chicago, Illinois. The old-time Gandy Dancer did his work by hand. His tools consisted of picks, shovels, ballast forks, and lining bars. In order to move heavy objects such as ties or rail, teamwork was required. Commonly songs were sung to pass the time. The songs or chants would have a specific beat to keep the gang working in unison. At certain points, the workers would lift together, allowing a few men to exert enough force to move heavy sections of track or rails. As they moved, they appeared to "dance"... giving the second portion of their nickname. Noah couldn't recall specific songs, but he did recall singing them.

The Flora Depot was built in 1917 by the B&O Railroad. Noah began working for B&O shortly after its completion. Recently, the building barely escaped demolition due to disrepair, but thanks to a group of local residents with ties to the railroad, fundraising began and it survived. Today, the depot is restored, serving as a museum, office space, and community gathering place. Noah would be proud.

Needless to say, Noah worked hard. His job was very labor intensive, and he was gone for long periods at a time. I would describe what he did as one of the most masculine, macho, testosterone-driven jobs around. It wasn't for the weak or faint of heart.

On one of my visits to him, he politely and modestly asked, "Would you like to see what I used to do as a pastime before my eyes and hands gave out?" I told him I would be honored. He struggled to lift himself from his recliner, grabbed his walker, and slowly made his way to the spare bedroom. I thought what surely awaited me behind that door would be an assortment of deer heads on the wall, a massive gun collection, or perhaps boxing trophies. That's the kind of guy I assumed he was.

He walked over to a large old-fashioned trunk and slowly lifted the lid. To my surprise, it was full of beautiful, handmade quilts! They were every color, pattern, and design imaginable. He had more in the closet and some in another room. That was his pastime. He quilted. He took those bear-paw hands, cut tiny pieces of fabric, and sewed them together until a masterpiece was made. No way, I thought, did this rough, tough, burly man quilt. But he did, and they were beautiful. I couldn't have been more surprised. This was a passion that for him spanned a lifetime. What a unique individual.

What I Learned

For years and years now, television, schools, churches, and people in general have been trying to teach us to be accepting, non-judgmental, and tolerant. Today, we have male flight attendants and women contractors. The day of men doing "men only" things and women doing "women only" things are gone. In spite of knowing this, I still put him in a category. We really shouldn't stereotype people. Anyone is capable of doing anything. Noah was proof of that. This was an eye-opening experience and it taught me that the sky is the limit for everyone.

Mary

After one of our home health patients passed away, the family called and asked if we would like to have the left over medical equipment. They had no use for it and would like to see it help someone else. We gladly accepted the donation as many of our patients are in need of walkers, wheelchairs, and hospital beds but are unable to afford them. One of our nurses asked if I would like to travel to Fairfield with them to help load it up and bring it back. I had never met the patient whose equipment we were accepting, but I was happy to ride along and help. The house was in Fairfield, the town where my grandma had always lived.

I loved my grandma and she loved me. The relationship was so important to me as a little girl growing into a woman. Her name was Mary Mitchell and she was the quintessential grandmother. Envision a tattered, worn apron tied around the waist of a woman who loved to spoil her grandchildren. I can still remember her house in nearly every detail. We spent every Sunday visiting her when I was young. Her kitchen always smelled of home-cooked meals. The Sunday menu was nearly always fried chicken and mashed potatoes with milk gravy. She would always me save the crunchy bits of chicken that stuck to the iron skillet just before making her world-class gravy. Now that was a treat.

I can still see and feel her warm, wrinkled, and freckled hands. Her sense of humor was unsurpassed. She always saw the humorous side to a situation, no matter how bad it was. In my eyes she was saintly, even though she was known to tell an off-color joke from time to time.

Her basement contained two things that always amused me. She kept some "homemade, medicinal wine" which was a surprise to me since I was taught "alcohol shall not touch the lips of a good Christian woman." Also in that basement was a big trunk that held an assortment of clothes for playing dress up. Every Sunday I would descend into the private world of make believe and put on her costume jewelry, old dresses, and shoes of every size and color. Of course, a parade in front of everyone ensued.

On our way to get the medical appliances, I shared with my colleagues stories about my Grandma and what a special lady she was. As we entered Fairfield, we drove toward the street where she lived. Entering her neighborhood I felt a sense of sadness come over me, as I hadn't been back in years. Then, the most unbelievable thing happened. We pulled right into her driveway! The house where we were going was the very house my grandma used to live! I was so taken back that it took me longer to get out of the car than the others. My heart was beating hard and I wasn't sure I could go any further. After some time, I made my way up the steps and entered the house. A flood of emotion overcame me. It was as if I was ten years old again.

I could smell the chicken frying, hear her laugh, and see her reach out for me. I never made it five feet into the house before turning around and heading outside. I stood there in the yard with my hands on my knees barely able to breathe. The whole experience was Deja vu in every poignant sense of the word, complete with color, smells, sounds, and touch.

I was unable to reenter the house and simply sat in the car, amazed at my inability to embrace what had just happened. If I had been prepared, it might have turned out differently. To date, it has been the most overwhelming experience of my life.

What I Learned

What I learned from this experience simply confirms what I already knew. The depths of true, unconditional love are forever lasting and unmeasurable. I adored my grandma and even forty years after saying goodbye to her, I found my love remained just as tangible and just as deep. Some things in life simply never go away. Grandma, if you are reading this, and I know you are, I want you to know how much I miss you and wish I had some of your fried chicken. And yes, I am still a good girl. I think you would be proud. I love you.

Denise Plumlee-
Tadlock
2014

Evelyn

What I admired most about Evelyn was her ability to maintain a positive outlook on life, in spite of the fact that she had not left her house in months. She lived alone and was truly homebound, yet she was resourceful enough to find ways to obtain her groceries and pay her bills. Evelyn barely reached five feet tall, but had a determination that made her size insignificant. She was ill, but it was her household and she was in charge.

Both of her lower legs were badly swollen and ulcerated. Twice a week visits to her home were necessary to apply a special wrap to the ulcers called Unna Boots. Unna Boot is a special gauze bandage, about four inches wide and ten yards long, which can be used for the treatment of venous stasis ulcers and other venous insufficiencies of the leg. The gauze is impregnated with a thick, creamy mixture of zinc oxide and calamine to promote healing. I would dip the Unna Boot in water until it became like an old plaster cast. The Unna Boot was then wound around her leg until the entire ten yards was used.

As you can imagine, after months of twice weekly visits, we

became very familiar with each other. I learned a lot about her and her past, and she enjoyed hearing about my children and their school accomplishments. I looked forward to my visits with her.

As the months wore on and 1987 was drawing to a close, Christmas began to approach. She worried about what she could do as she was unable to leave her house, and unable to stand in the kitchen long enough to make "goodie baskets". I assured her that everyone would understand and she shouldn't worry about trying to buy gifts for anyone this year. She needed to concentrate on getting better. I helped her set out a few decorations and give her home the appearance of having the Christmas spirit.

The last time I went to see her before the Christmas break, she just glowed when she opened the door. I knew something was up. After finishing the long process of leg wrapping, she said she had something for me. I was surprised as I had no idea how she had managed to get out and go shopping. Well, she didn't.

She reached behind her chair and pulled out a bag and presented it to me with the biggest smile on her face. I'm ashamed to admit this now, but I was stunned and disappointed at what it contained. Inside was an old, yellowed, full slip, and not even close to my size. I managed to contain my less than enthusiastic reception and graciously thank her.

She then proceeded to tell me the story of the slip. About forty years earlier, she had babysat for a little boy who grew up to be a successful doctor. One year at Christmas time, she was presented with this slip as a gift from his parents. Back in the day, lingerie was expensive and considered a very luxurious gift. She was so proud of this gift that she kept it tucked away in a special drawer all those years. The slip was her most prized possession, and she wanted me to have it. The more I thought about how insulted I was at such a perceived thoughtless gift, the more ashamed I became of myself. Presenting me with the slip was the highlight of her Christmas season, as well as mine. I'm not sure I have ever received a gift since that I was so honored to have.

What I Learned

It took a while for me to fully appreciate what I had been given. I think of that slip often when I am desperately trying to think of just the perfect gift for someone. It seems to me that we put way too much emphasis on the expense of the gift, the brand name, or that it was bought at an exclusive department store. None of those things really matter. I don't know who said it first, Santa Claus, or William Shakespeare, but he was right. It's not the gift but the thought that counts. I found that to be so true. As you can see, thirty years after I received the gift, I still have it. I'm not even sure where my gifts are or what they were, from just last year. We should constantly try to remind ourselves of what's truly important.

Denise Plumlee-Tadlock
2014

Harold

In his prime, Harold was a rough and tough character; a perfect blend of Clint Eastwood and John Wayne. True to his character type, he worked hard and played even harder. His one true
love was his motorcycle. He especially loved the roar of a fully
dressed, top of the line Harley Davidson. Even though he had a
car, he rode his bike for business, and he road for pleasure. He
could often be spotted cruising along the wide open countryside
or onto a heavy, congested interstate. Often his road trips led
him to some place unique and different, usually a locally owned
coffee shop for sandwich and cup of coffee. This was all before
the accident.

Harold's family had been life-long oil people. His family
hadn't always been wealthy, but in 1939, Clay County experienced an oil boom, which turned his quiet country town with
955 residents into somewhat of a lucrative and fast-paced city.

In March of 1939, Pure Oil Company drilled the first of its
mega-empire oil well on what was called the old Weiler place.
(It's still pumping today, seventy-five years later) Following that
first oil well, hundreds followed. A single oil well often pumped

up to 1200 barrels of oil a day. What had always been a sleepy, laid-back community was suddenly a hubbub of activity, but more importantly, money. And lots of it. Dirt-poor farmers that had never owned more than the shirt on their backs were suddenly driving shiny new Oldsmobile's. Old timers that are still alive and remember the boom stated that people came from miles away to watch the activity. Some land owners reportedly charged each car a nickel to park on their property for the day.

In its prime, nearly everyone in the surrounding area worked for Pure Oil in some capacity. The demand for workers was so great that Pure Oil built its own camp in Clay County. The camp resembled a little community within itself. Many of the employees lived in this camp, where the entire collection of houses all looked alike. They even had their own baseball team that traveled around the United States and competed against, and won, some big name baseball teams.

But, as true with most things in life, everything must come to an end. The rags to riches story was good while it lasted, but in 1960 Pure Oil found a way to reduce expenditures by contracting out work instead of using their own employees. 200 men lost their jobs that year so without company housing, many simply went back home. The boom was over.

But Harold continued to prosper. He was not only a landowner that had stuck oil, he was a Pure Oil employee too. He banded pipe for the oil company which allowed the oil to move on down the line. Life was good for Harold until one evening a truck pulled out in front of him while riding his bike. That was the last time he walked.

As a young nurse, I was nervous about taking care of him. He was paralyzed from mid-chest down, had been bed bound for years, and wore a urinary catheter. I didn't know how to relate to him. I dreaded going there because it was such a sad case. He couldn't feed himself, had very minimal use of his arms, and had nothing to look forward to. And his poor wife. She was bound to live a life of depression and darkness right along with him. His life was over; he had no enjoyment, and merely existed. Or so I thought.

The first time I saw Harold, I did as the written instructions said: go to the front door, knock, and go on in. After knocking, I went inside and shouted "Hello, Hello" but I got no response. Soon I heard a noise coming from the back of the house. I slowly crept down the hall to where a light was on. I heard the sounds of two people talking, or more like fighting. I was worried what I'd find. I opened the bedroom door and there was Harold and his wife, in full battle over a game of gin rummy, in which Harold had just "ginned". Someone had made Harold a special card holder for oversized cards. He was able to use his hands and arms enough to actively participate in the game, and there certainly was nothing wrong with his brain. As I walked in, he had just said to his wife "Take that you old bag" to which she replied, "I'd win every time too if I cheated like you". I stood there in astonishment. They were laughing, living, and loving.

As time went by and I became more familiar with Harold and his wife and felt comfortable to venture into some very personal issues. I told him how surprised I was at how self-sufficient he was when I first met him and that I expected with his level of disability to be angry and unable to care for himself.

I will never forget the way he looked at me. It was as if to say "you poor, sweet, young, naïve person". He let me know that just because his legs were no longer of use to him, his heart and soul were very much alive. As one might expect, he did spend some time in denial and being angry. But with help from some very good people, he was able to move on and live his life to the fullest. He truly enjoyed every day, became wholeheartedly engrossed in the daytime soaps, still conducted some oil business from his bed, and lived his life as if he were whole. Harold was an inspiration to me. He truly opened my eyes to the possibilities that exist with sheer grit and determination.

What I Learned

It would be safe for me to say that I learned more about the human spirit from Harold than from any other patient. As a young inexperienced nurse, I had a tendency to place everyone with a particular disease neatly together in organized boxes. Little did I know that for people with handicaps, limitations, disabilities, whatever term you choose to use, there are no boundaries. Someone who is deaf can still hear the remarkable melody of a Mozart concerto, the blind can vividly see a beautiful Arizona sunset, and a person with no legs can still live a very fulfilling life. For most of us, our limitations are only in our mind. I want to thank you, Harold, for being a strong mentor to me and for not allowing me to go through my entire adult life with blinders on.

Laura

Laura was born and raised during the depression. Most people who lived through that trying time can remember how the world felt to them. It was cold, uncaring, and many people lost everything they had. But sometimes there are unforeseen, surprising outcomes that arise from disasters or unplanned tragedies.

Like many people born into the depression generation, Laura knew early on that anything she was to get out of life she had to fight for. Once it was obtained, she had to fight to keep it. She was a bit of a risk-taker, but when you have nothing, the risk of what you have to lose is less. She told me that during her young adult years and the years she was raising her family, she did what she could to bring in money to feed her four children. She sold Avon, Tupperware, and raised pedigree dogs and sold puppies. Her favorites were German Shepherds, Boston Terriers, and Basset Hounds. Laura also had a Jersey cow that was milked every day with the milk, cream, and butter being sold to neighbors. There were also chickens and eggs peddled. There was never money for extra things, and Laura relayed to me how she managed to get her daughter shoes for the prom in 1969.

In the early days with rustic farm machinery, the two-row corn picker often missed much of the corn and left it to lie in the ground and eventually rot. When the temperature dipped below freezing, she got into her 1940 Ford grain truck and drove over the rough frozen field. She walked and threw corn into the back of the grain truck until she had enough corn to sell to purchase the shoes. Love can conquer a lot of things, even poverty.

Whether it was the depression aftermath or just her personality, she was often stubborn and obstinate. She had her opinion of how things should go, and generally liked to have the last word. Even though she was a challenging patient, something in me envied her tenacity. You sure didn't push her around or force her into anything without her approval. Even at her advanced age, she clung onto as much control as possible.

Caring for her tried my patience. As a health care professional, I felt I knew what was best for her. However, an argument nearly always ensued when a new idea was offered or a suggestion for a better or safer way to do something was discussed. "A pill organizer? Why do I need that? I have all of my medicine in this shoe box," she would say.

"Yes, yes you do," I would reply, "but it also contains outdated meds, discontinued meds, pills mixed with other pills in one little bottle, not to mention the general state of confusion this brings about such as remembering when to take the medications, which ones, and at what time."

We argued over the need for oxygen. "I don't need that! Give it to somebody that does." Or, "I'm not taking my Insulin anymore. It's too expensive so I'm just going to control my diabetes with diet and exercise." I replied that was a pretty tall order, considering she took insulin four times a day and was unable to walk more than twenty-five feet. But nothing I did or said seemed to break through the obstinate barrier that she seemed to have. No matter how completely and professionally I explained the circumstance, she remained steadfast. I had been a home health nurse for twenty years and I had previously persuaded many rather unchanging individuals to make positive changes to improve their health. Sometimes it was difficult but I eventually got the job done. Not so with Laura. She was a defiant, immovable, rock. So, with a defeatist attitude, I waved the white flag and decided to take one final approach.

With a pleading, exasperated voice, I took her hand and looked into her dulled, yet determined eyes and said, "Will you try it one time, just for me? Please, Mom."

At this point of surrender it became clear to me. As her child, I was never going to get her to take me or her health seriously. While I would be making a point about a potentially deadly Insulin reaction, she would interrupt me to ask if I'd heard from my brother Dan lately. So I did what I should have done much earlier. I asked one of my colleagues to take over her care. To my relief, she listened to every word she said. She allowed the new nurse to organize her medications, get her oxygen levels back on track and she began to take care of her diabetes. From that point on, I cared for her only under the role of daughter.

What I Learned

Much can be said about the difficulty one faces when suddenly the child becomes the parent, or in this case, the educator. In this particular circumstance, it was obvious my mother was never going to view me as anything but her child. It didn't matter how many degrees I had, or how many awards or accomplishments I had decorating my wall; to my mother I was perpetually twelve years old. I don't think that's necessarily a bad thing, nor am I offended by her seemingly lack of recognition of my skills as "super-nurse". I'm just glad we found the correct combination of medical care for her to benefit.

Lorene

This is a lesson that I would encourage you to read, and then read again. Read it until it is imbedded into your brain. Never allow yourself to be placed in such an irreversible place of torment.

Lorene lived in a neat, older farmhouse in the northern part of our county. Even though it was neat and orderly, nearly everything in the house was very old. Most things like lights, plumbing, and electric, worked some of the time, others things only occasionally.

Lorene lived in her charming rural house with her husband of many years. She had recently suffered a heart attack and I was there to help her recuperate quickly and with the most positive results possible. The date of that fateful day I don't recall but from the outcome, it must have been the day after Thanksgiving.

As soon as I arrived, I had a belly pain that I knew wasn't going to wait until I finished assessing Lorene and then drive twenty-five miles back to my office. So without suspicion, I asked Lorene where the bathroom was, that I needed to "wash my hands" before starting. She explained that it was right down the hall and that there were plenty of towels beside the sink. I, of course, knew that hand washing wasn't the reason for my urgent bathroom request, but felt no need to go into detail with my patient. Some things are better left unsaid.

Well, without being overly descriptive, let me just say that what I expelled was like nothing I had ever seen. It made a complete loop around the bowl and if I'm not mistaken, even overlapped itself.

As I sat there reaching for the toilet paper, Lorene shouted from the living room, "Barb, I hope you're not using the toilet, it's broken."

What?! Are you kidding me? This couldn't be happening! Beads of sweat broke out on my forehead and I felt faint. What am I going to do? In my desperation to think through this predicament, I noticed a window. That's it! If I can get it open and hoist myself out, then I can belly-crawl past the front window, past the poor, unsuspecting homeowners, and to my car.

"Why oh why," I cried, "couldn't it have been like any other day, not one that would be talked about in the ladies circle in church for Sunday's to come?" I felt a rush of panic come over me and my flight or fight self-preservation kicked in. Perhaps I could just exit the bathroom, get my bag, walk out, and drive away. But then I would have to quit my job and move. So, I did what any self-respecting person would do. I washed my hands, straightened my hair, closed the lid, and went out and performed the best darned assessment known to mankind. I then told her to have a nice day and without a word, I left. I just left. This was not my proudest moment.

I'm not sure what I should have done, or what any fairly responsible person would have done. Did I think they wouldn't notice? Or maybe I could just get another nurse to go for the next three months and I would never have to face them again. Of course, there would always be the possibility that I would turn an isle in the grocery store some day and be nose to nose with them. At any rate, I chose the cowardly route, but made another visit the following week as if nothing happened. Hopefully, after several decades, I've been forgiven. Most likely not forgotten, but at least forgiven.

What I Learned

I don't care how fancy the house is in which you live, or how modern your office building is, never, and I mean never, take anything such as flushing for granted. If you are somewhere and find yourself needing to "wash your hands," by all means, test the equipment first. It may just save you thirty years of hiding behind a display of canned goods.

Jack and Carol

If there ever lived two more unique people than Jack and Carol, I don't know who they are. They were below average in intelligence and the health care needs of the pair were multiple. The Health Department found itself in a never ending cycle of recurring treatments.

Jack was a very large man. He wore overalls every day and probably didn't have anything else, nor did he want it. His overalls never fully buttoned at the sides as his girth spilled out far beyond the denim's capacity. His hair was long and never washed nor combed. I'm not sure the last time he had a bath, but it was long before I began seeing him. He was mostly wheelchair-bound due to his size. Jack huffed and puffed when trying to stand and pivot from one chair to another. The nurses treated him for stasis ulcers, or open draining sores on his legs. These were due to years of medical neglect. He had no way to get to the doctor so he would treat himself with home remedies. He didn't have any money and never would. Yet, there wasn't a time I saw him that he wasn't smiling.

Carol pretty much mirrored Jack, except in size. She was a tiny lady, barely tipping the scales at 100 pounds. I doubted her hair had seen a brush in years. As far as physical capability, Carol was relatively healthy, just mentally challenged. Her hygiene was lacking too, but she seemed unaware. One of my nurses had been a cosmetologist in her past and would sometimes take her hair and nail supplies on her visit. After Jack was tended to, Rhonda would break out the nail polish and hairs bows and go to work. This thrilled Carol because in spite of her appearance and mentality, she desired to be pretty. Carol was also a hugger. Each visit she wanted to hug and show her gratitude. If we weren't careful, before we knew it, she'd have us around the neck with our heads touching, side-by-side, giving us the biggest warmest welcome possible. The problem with that was Carol's continual head lice infestation. As hard as we tried to keep our distance, she always managed to show her affection.

She used to come into the Health Department occasionally when she wanted to show off her babies. Carol had a teddy bear and a doll that she took everywhere. She had a rickety baby carrier and she gingerly carried the bear and doll around as if they were real. Carol would frequent garage sales and thrift shops looking for new clothes for them and while money was tight, the bear and doll were always dressed to the nines to match the current season.

The home they lived in is nearly indescribable. The yard was completely covered by six-foot weeds and lazy dogs. There was a narrow dirt path that led to the porch. The porch was a maze of broken, rotten boards that challenged each visitor that made way to the door. Once inside, it was hard to take it all in. Boxes, papers, boards, mice droppings, and junk littered nearly every square inch of the floor. In fact, not only was the floor covered, most of the carpet was damp and squished when walked upon. The mounds of litter went from floor to ceiling. Everything was brown, dirty, and smelly. There were dozens of cats and kittens in the house, all of varying ages. They were all sickly with sore matted eyes, missing fur, and red, angry bottoms. The smell of animal feces was everywhere and there were even dead kittens in one corner. The house had neither running water nor electricity. There was no way to cook nor do dishes if they had any. In the corner of the bedroom was a five gallon bucket that was used as a make-shift toilet. When it became full, it was removed and re-placed with another empty bucket.

Carol would meet me at the door and readily show me to the bedroom where Jack awaited his wound care. We would wind through a brown, dirty maze and finally enter the bedroom. Again, air supply was low just from the amount of content in the room. Jack was lying in a filthy bed under sheets that hadn't seen a washer in months, if not years. He had an illuminating, electric beer sign on the wall just over his head that read "SEX DRIVE". The sign had arrows pointing in all directions.

As I attempted a sterile dressing change on his leg, Carol would frantically try to stave off a hoard of kittens who clamored over him, his leg, and my supplies. They were everywhere. One time during his wound care she said nonchalantly, "Oh Jack, the cat shit in the bed again." With that she took a previously used paper towel and wiped it, mostly just smearing the feces over the bed sheets. I recall one time after leaving their house, I had to stop about two miles down the road, get out of my car, and vomit.

Eventually his wounds healed and he was discharged. He died shortly after that as did Carol. Everything seems to be erased from their past, as evidenced by the complete collapse that once was the structure of their house. Though we never seemed to have a deep connection, I miss them all the same.

What I Learned

My visits with Jack and Carol were exhausting. They were medically difficult, but they were also enchanting. In my description of them, as well as their home, I was simply trying to paint a picture, not pass judgment. I learned thirty years ago that I can't expect everyone to live as I do. We are all unique individuals with individual tastes. What is important to me is not necessarily important to someone else. And no one is particularly right or wrong. It also isn't fair to judge someone who doesn't have the mental, physical, or financial capacity to change their lot in life. No amount of teaching was going to change who they were. They were for the most part, completely unaware that anyone might find the way they lived appalling. They always welcomed me with warmth and graciousness.

It was with Jack and Carol that I learned my job was simply to do the best I could. I could not move mountains. And, in spite of our differences, we had a great relationship. They were a delightful couple. They were my first experience as a young home health nurse with such poverty. I learned from them not to look down in judgment at people less fortunate than me. They were doing the best they could. They deserved just as much of my time and respect as the next person; maybe more so.

Denise Plumlee-Tadlock
2014

William

William and his wife, Louise, had been married longer than most people are alive. Louise would smile and state that she couldn't remember a time that she wasn't married. She took her job as being Mrs. William very seriously, for that was her chosen career. She took care of her husband and their three children. Louise never doubted her contribution to her family, and working outside the home was never an option. While many women today struggle with trying to take care of the home as well as "bringing home the bacon", Louise never concerned herself with paying jobs. When William fell ill and became bedbound, she cared for him as most of us can only dream of being cared for. It was her job and none but hers.

William was equally proud of his role as the sole financial provider for the family. He spent his entire career working in the one thriving factory that Flora had, the International Shoe Factory. Flora was lucky to acquire this factory, as the supply of employment opportunities locally had run its course. The B&O Railway was a large employer but they had no vacancies. In fact, none were to be found anywhere.

I was privileged to see a February 22, 1923 Flora Journal-Record, which William still possessed. It was an interesting article about the potential acquisition, which stated that if the residents of Flora could produce $75,000 and a building site, the International Shoe Factory would agree to locate one of its standard factories here. The city would supply the building site, but the residents had to front the money. The campaign slogan to obtain the factory was "Are you for or against Flora? There is no neutral ground." The residents seemed to be split into two classes: boosters and knockers. The boosters, of course, wholeheartedly supported the grand effort to secure the potential business while the knockers were opposed. Thankfully, the knockers were a very small minority.

The city was asking for each household to pledge $200 toward the $75,000. One woman who was interviewed after she paid her $200 stated that she had several children, some reaching young adulthood. There were no jobs available and they would have nowhere to work. Even though she didn't have the money to spare, she felt she had no choice but to join forces with her other neighbors and try to secure a future for her children.

The article went on to mention that "employees of the shoe factory shall consist of both males and females between the ages of sixteen and thirty-five years. The probable ratio would be 60% male and 40% female." My how times have changed. William also mentioned that the factory workers stitched together leather and camouflage-colored boots that were shipped to our young men and women in the armed forces in Vietnam.

A small, but very determined, group of local residents did indeed move a mountain. In 1923, the coveted International Shoe Factory opened its doors. Unfortunately the shoe factory closed in 1966, but only after providing a good living to hundreds of families in Flora for 43 years.

William worked at the shoe factory and raised his entire family on income derived from the job. He loved to talk about his career on my visits and I enjoyed his stories. Even though he was bedbound and most days battled chronic pain, he made the most of his time and was doted on by his loving wife. One afternoon as I made my visit to him, I was startled by what I saw. He was white as a ghost, his skin was very cold, and he was barely conscious. As I pulled the sheet back to examine him, the bed was full of blood. Blood seemed to be everywhere. He was bleeding rectally and had lost a life-threatening amount. I immediately called for the ambulance and had him rushed to the hospital.

Upon arrival, they began pumping him with blood as quickly as possible. Even though he was in critical condition and remained critical, his life had been saved. I waited for a couple of days before stopping by the hospital to see him, as I felt he needed time to rest and recuperate.

In my mind's eye, this was how I saw my visit to William and Louis playing out in the hospital. I would slowly open the door and smile with my hands clasped tightly over my heart. The heavens would open and rays of intense bright light would filter down from the sky. A heavenly choir would be singing and the presence of love and gratitude would be overwhelming. In a phrase, their Earthly Savior had arrived and I would be forced to modestly accept their accolades. Louise would genuflect at my presence and I would insist that I was a mere mortal too. That's what I thought would happen, but it's not what I got. Not even close. Louise came rushing across the room when she saw it was me. She got as close to my face as she could get and she was furious. Her face turned red and I could tell her heart was pounding.

She lifted her boney little finger to my face and said, "I am so angry at you. This is all your fault. Look at him lying there. His body is swollen and barely recognizable. If it hadn't been for you, he'd be gone by now." I didn't know what to say. I just stood in the doorway, too stunned to move as she walked back to his bedside.

What I Learned

What just happened? I quickly did the math in my head. Let's see: William and Louise loved each other: Check. Louise found purpose in her role as William's caregiver: Check. As per my training I did a quick assessment, found the patient to be in a critical state hovering near death, acted promptly by summoning emergency personnel, and saved his life: Check. Then, how could things have gone so badly off course?

Many years ago I shared an office with a social worker who labeled me a "pacifier". In other words, all I want is for everyone to get along and be happy. The thought of someone being so angry and upset with me was nearly more that I could take.

They were both elderly but still very much in love. Why would she not want me to do everything possible to save his life? Later, she disclosed to me that he had been in ill health for years and was in pain every day. Mentally, they were both prepared for when the time came. They knew they would be together again someday, so William leaving his earthly body was something they were very much prepared to face. I simply didn't see it that way. He still enjoyed life and she found her purpose in caring for him. We never discussed just "letting him go". That's not what I thought either of them would want.

Caring for William was before the concept of Hospice, so as nurses we never had end-of-life conversations with our patients. Instead, we just tried to perpetually cure everyone and heal the world. I went over the disturbing scenario over and over, and each time arrived at the same conclusion. In retrospect, do you know what I would have done differently? Not one thing. I swore, through my Hippocratic Oath, many years ago to practice medicine honestly. Even knowing the outcome that Louise would probably take it out on me, I still would not have changed a thing. I simply had to learn that there will be times when not everyone will be happy with me. There was no way I could have just pulled the sheet back up, looked away, and not responded. I've always done my job as honestly as I can, and even with everything done appropriately, sometimes you win and sometimes you lose.

Leon

After months of treating a small non-healing ulcer, Leon had the words spoken to him that no man on Earth ever wants to hear. "Leon, the report came back. You have cancer of the penis." As you can imagine, that was a devastating and traumatizing diagnosis. In fact, he had difficulty speaking of it, acknowledging it, or discussing it. The cancerous area was on the tip and the only treatment was surgical removal of the malignant area. What an emasculating devastation to a man. Even though the surgery was a partial excision or removal of the cancerous area, he felt his life as he knew it, both as a man and a husband, was about to change.

Leon was a very likable and well-known man and his wife, Linda, was a beautiful "southern belle". He spent most of his adult life as a successful insurance salesman in North Carolina. His outgoing personality and striking good looks aided his rapid rise to the top of his profession. While selling insurance was what he did for a living, it wasn't his love or his passion. His heart belonged to The Southerners. Leon was one of four who made up the gospel quartet named The Southerners who performed for nearly fifteen years in and around Rocky Mount and Roanoke Rapids, North Carolina. Leon was personal friends with groups such as Hovie Lister and the Statesmen, The Blackwood Brothers, and The Oakridge Boys. On the weekends, Linda and her "Widows on Weekends" group, made up of the quartet wives, would get together and enjoy each other's company while the men traveled and sang.

While Leon was still in his prime, he developed a series of neuromuscular disorders called: focal dystonia, spasmodic torticollis, and blepharospasm. This caused a disfiguration of the head and neck, forcing him to give up both his thriving insurance business and his singing. Over the course of his treatments, Leon and Dr. Joel Perlmutter, a research neurologist and surgeon, had become good friends. When Leon died, he donated his brain to Dr. Perlmutter for research.

When Leon and Linda decided to retire, they chose to leave the Carolinas and come back to the peaceful, rural, southern Illinois family home. Linda loved it there and thrived, but continued to miss the hospitality that only comes from the Carolinas and playing hostess to one of her splendid tea parties. Leon found a new career hosting a big-band era music show on our local radio station. His radio personality name was Russ Paul. His disability was unseen over the radio waves and he was loved by everyone.

Leon's referral was made to me through one of our very large hospitals in the St. Louis, Missouri area. He chose to receive his surgery in St. Louis in order to obtain the most advanced and latest in technical procedures. Larger hospitals are able to provide so much more in the way of expertise and specialists than can our small twenty-bed hospital. As Leon's nurses were preparing to send him home, I received a phone call from the hospital asking for at least one follow-up visit. He was coming home with a catheter and the reason for my visit was to remove it. The hospital hoped to make his trip home as painless and uncomplicated as possible. Sounded simple enough.

I went to Leon's house the evening of his arrival home. Both Leon and Linda were nervous, and rightfully so. When I was finished with my visit, what transpired as I was about to leave his home was a travesty. Never, ever should anything like this occur.

Neither Leon nor Linda had seen the actual surgical wound or been prepared for the extent of the surgery. We made small talk as I was preparing for the catheter removal. Both were in the room as I pulled the bandage away. Much to the shock of everyone present, there had been a complete excision of the penis. In fact, the wound was actually concave, or hollowed or rounded inward like the inside of a bowl. With great care I removed the catheter and covered his fresh surgical wound. That discovery in itself should have been enough, but what happened next defied all logic.

I gathered my supplies and asked Leon if he had any questions for me before I left. He said no, he guessed he didn't. I walked to the door and instructed him to call me if he had any problems; otherwise he was to have a follow-up visit to his surgeon in two weeks. I said goodbye and as I reached for the door Leon said, "Barb, how am I supposed to go to the bathroom?"

I stood there in horror and asked him to repeat himself. I said, "Didn't anyone talk to you about that?" He stated that no one had said a word. I didn't know what to do. I was a young nurse in the middle of nowhere and I sure didn't know either.

Here was a man who had just been given a life-changing surgery, and no one spoke to him about how to care for himself now that his anatomy was altered. Don't you think someone should have mentioned to him what he needed to do in order to urinate now that he didn't have a penis? Further, they should have addressed what would happen between Leon and his wife. Their shared intimacy as a married couple was gone. No one talked about that either. At a minimum they should have had a social worker or therapist to speak to them about how their lives would be different and to help them get dialog started. They received nothing. Imagine the panic that must have been in his mind at that moment. I told him truthfully that I honestly didn't know what he was supposed to do. I would try to get in touch with his doctor as soon as I got back to my office and would call him the moment I knew something.

I must have driven like a mad woman on my way back as I felt time was rather critical. I called the discharging hospital and gave an earful to someone who probably had nothing to do with our current situation. What a complete and utter travesty that this man, this couple, was sent home with no counseling, or more importantly and more urgent, information on how he was supposed to relieve his bladder.

I sure didn't know. I couldn't even recall at that moment where the bladder sphincter was, if it had been removed, or if he would even have bladder control. I remember being so angry with his doctors and the hospital. I guess the primary issue was taken care of, the cancer was gone, but my goodness, what an injustice to this wonderful couple. This is a perfect example of how not to deliver medical care.

What I Learned

What I learned from this patient is simple. There is an expression that has been around for a hundred years, but it never held as much truth as with Leon and Linda. Bigger is not always better. Under the guidance of their local physician they chose to go to a large city hospital where the latest in medical advancement and technology is un-rivaled. But Leon got lost in the system. He was no longer a person with a heart, feelings, and a family. He was only a number on the roster for that day. Together Leon, Linda, and I made it through, but there had been so much un-necessary stress and grief. When Leon's "fall from grace" occurred, as he was to put it, it became a reminder to all of us to count our blessings for each healthy day we have. As the disability took over his life, so could it ours at any moment. Let us never forget that.

Denise Plumlee-Tadlock
2014

Walter

Everyone loved Walter. He was a soft-spoken, southern gentleman. His calm, unflappable demeanor instantly drew people to him. To describe Walter in a word, he was "grandfatherly". I don't recall anyone having an unkind word to say about him, or disliking him in the least. He and his wife had been married for many years when she suddenly became ill. Before he had time to react, she was gone. While she tended to the general oversight of the house, Walter felt his responsibility, as many of the men in his era did, was to provide financially for his family. He had been widowed for many years the time I first met him, and he described how quickly he had to learn to do what his wife had always done: cook, do laundry, and pay bills.

His doctor referred him to us because he was lost with his medications. Polypharmacy is a word we use to describe a situation in which a patient, generally an older person, takes multiple medications, as did Walter. We were called to assist Walter in teaching him how to organize his medicines and take them correctly.

With the written description above, I think you will be as surprised as I was when you learn what happened next. On our first visit, we sat in the living room and he described to me the passing of his wife and how it had affected him. He was tearful, and rightfully so. Walter was still grieving for her. We made small talk about what he did for a living, what his hobbies were, and what his plans were for the future. After a while, I suggested we walk into the kitchen so that we could tackle the task of organizing his pills. He was agreeable and thought having help was a good idea and he was glad his doctor had suggested it.

Before we stood up to walk to the kitchen, Walter said something odd. He said he wanted me to know that he was often unbalanced and unsteady on his feet. He would sometimes stagger and often appear as if he'd had too much to drink. He wanted to apologize in advance if during our walk to the kitchen, he suddenly lost his balance and accidently touched my breast. I laughed, thanked him for the warning, but told him not to worry, everything would be all right.

With that we stood up and started for the kitchen, and wouldn't you know it. He began to stagger and his arms flailed about as if fighting for his life. I'll be darned if he didn't lose his balance and sure enough, his hand fell right over my left breast! I could barely believe what had just happened. What are the odds of that happening? I asked myself. In his defense he gave me fair warning, but this soft-spoken gentleman caught me totally off guard. I told him not to worry, and then I ended up apologizing to him.

What I Learned

When this incident first happened, I was angry, hurt, and I'll admit, I was disgusted by his behavior. What kind of a man was he? Well, before we look at what kind of man he was at that moment, let's look at who he was before; before all the ravages that can befall an aging person, before he was left without his wife, his memory, his dignity, and before his life became a fulltime process of organizing pills and doctors' appointments. In my first couple of paragraphs I described a loving husband and a gentle soul that was loved by everyone. The person who once stood so tall among his friends and family, was not the man I met that day. That man would have never exhibited such offensive behavior. Loving, gentle, and kind, that's what kind of man he was.

Denise Plumlee-Tadlock
2014

Marvin

It was actually Marvin's mother, Elsie, that I saw as a patient. Even though I can't recall the exact nature of her illness, I vividly remember her house and her son. He had temporarily come back home to help with his mother's recuperation. Elsie introduced me to Marvin and said that he would be here only for a few days as his work would not allow him much time away. I recall Marvin being handsome and having the demeanor of aloofness and importance.

Elsie was a pretty elderly lady with "chemically-assisted auburn hair". Her home was full of knick-knacks, antiques, and collectables from all over. I recall there being lots of primary colors; red, yellow, green, and blue. She apparently had a love for loud and vivid colors. She was pleasant during my interview and only stopped smiling long enough to talk. Marvin sat quietly in the background, allowing his mother the respect of answering my never-ending questions, even though he knew some of them may not be completely correct.

My daughter, Elizabeth, taken in 1998, the year
we made Frank's chicken and noodles.

Part of the B&O Railroad that Noah laid as foreman of his section gang.

The original oil pump that started the
massive oil boom of Clay County in 1939.

Standing in the abandoned location where
Jack and Carol's house was eventually demolished.

Leon and Linda Davidson.

My grandma's house and home to the finest
fried chicken and milk gravy ever made.

My son, Robby, posing by his
"rookie of the year" trophy in 1991.

Not Marvin, but Marvin's half brother and my
"knight in shining armor" Bob Tackitt.

The 1994 Mustang that made that fateful trip through Tick Ridge.

The old shoe factory in Flora, now closed and abandoned.

Sheila with three of her sisters, Connie, Kathy, and Debbie.

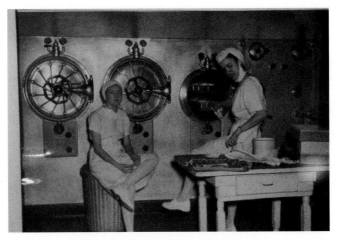

Jan Phillips (on left) and nursing
supervisor autoclaving instruments, circa 1948.

Three of the hand pieced quilts purchased from Bessie.

The old poultry house in Flora, IL. Proof that dreams can come true.

My mom, Betty Mitchell Eckelberry, and me on Mother's Day in 2009.

Marvin asked my name and if I was from around the area. He inquired into my in- laws, asking where we lived and a host of other questions that seemed to be more of a personal nature. However, when you live in a small rural area, it is not uncommon for the interviewer to answer as many questions as the person being interviewed. Once the patient and family fully understood who my "kin" is, then we could progress forward. To those who live in a large city this may seem very personal and intrusive, but believe me, in a rural community, it's just the way it is. And it's okay. "Yes, my father in-law lived south of Lincoln School, past Hangin' Rock and left at the T and yes, he was road commissioner for many years."

I explained that my husband was Bob Tackitt and we had been married for fifteen years. There were five siblings in Bob's family; two were pre-war and three more added after Bob's dad, Harvey, returned from WWII. Jack was the oldest followed by Hattie. One would describe Jack as being hard on the outside but soft on the inside. Hattie remained the matriarch of the family until her death. Both are gone now and sadly missed. Once Harvey returned from military duty, Patty was born, then Bob and finally Jim, who most of the family still call Jimmy. Every Sunday when "the folks" were still alive, each and every sibling would gather at the home place. They would cook, tend to the garden, help with mowing, and can what garden vegetables were ready or just spend time together. I have always appreciated that relationship. They were close and one sibling could always depend on another to help at an instant.

The evening after I made my visit to Elsie, I sat around the dining room table with Bob and our two children. I'm sure we had our usual meal of hamburger helper and applesauce, something I was guaranteed that both our kids, Elizabeth and Robby, would eat. While we were discussing the events of the day such as the impending piano recital and how the little league baseball

Rookie of the Year award was within Robby's grasp, the phone rang. I answered and the man on the phone said "Is this Barb Tackitt?" I said yes. He said "Are you the nurse that was at my Mom's house today?" Again, I confirmed that it was me. There was a pause and he asked, "Are you married to Bob Tackitt?" and I said yes for the third time. Then there was a longer pause and I was getting really uncomfortable. I finally asked, "Is there something I can help you with?" and he said, "I think your husband is my brother." I said "Excuse me? What did you say?" By this time Bob noticed that something disturbing was going on with the conversation and he kept saying, "Who is it? Who is it?" I was dumbfounded. I didn't know what to do or what to say. Finally I lowered the phone to my wildly beating heart and said, "This guy says he thinks he's your brother."

To my utter disbelief, Bob asked, "Oh, is that Marvin?"

My eyes widened as I replied "Who is Marvin?" I handed the phone over to Bob and they proceeded to have a thirty-minute conversation while I sat in stunned disbelief. Once he hung up the phone, he had a lot of explaining to do. Apparently, Harvey had been married to Elsie prior to his marriage to Margaret, resulting in Marvin. Harvey and Elsie divorced and Elsie took Marvin to live with her. Elsie remarried soon after her divorce and her new husband adopted Marvin. That was the end of Harvey and Marvin's relationship, and as a result, he was never spoken of or referred to again. I had no idea that Marvin existed until that moment.

What I Learned

I would be untruthful if I said that not knowing this dark secret didn't bother me. A woman likes to think that after being married to and knowing a man for seventeen years, that there is little left to know or learn. It's one of the things we women pride ourselves on, being the "be all" and the "end all" to our families. Come to find out, life still has surprises that often catch us unaware. Never assume you know everything about anyone or anything. And maybe that's a good thing.

Denise Plumlee-Tadlock
2014

Frank

Way out in the country, out where the "owls mate with the chickens" (cleaned-up version) lived Frank. He had once lived a satisfying and classic farm life. This included an assortment of farm equipment such as a tractor, plow, disc, planter, and combine. Additionally he had the usual farm animals, or livestock, such as cows for butchering and a scattering of chickens and guineas. Frank and his wife led a wonderful, long life and together raised their five children who are now grown and moved way. Frank and his wife would make rare trips into town to buy items their vegetable garden and animals couldn't supply.

I could personally relate to Frank and his wife, as they reminded me of my husband and me. They had obviously been very close and considered each other to be their best friend. Together they worked toward common goals and shared dreams. As you can imagine, after losing his wife of fifty-five years, Frank was lost, and his doctor felt he needed some extra attention due to his declining health and the realization that day after day would go by without anyone darkening his doorway. His doctor also thought a few home health visits might stimulate his recovery.

Franks wife was already gone when the two of us met. He was sad, lonely, and depressed. His physical health was much easier to treat than his mental health, which seemed to have a tight grip around his heart. I always tried to spend extra time with him if I could, as the simple act of conversation seemed to be of the most value. Long after my medical assessment was completed, I would ask him questions about his past and just let him reminisce. On one particular afternoon we were talking about his wife and what he missed most.

He tearfully said, "You know what I miss the most? I haven't had a good noodle since my wife died." Upon retelling this story to my husband that evening and commenting on his attachment to food, he remarked, "He hasn't had a good noodle since his wife died? What makes you think he's talking about food?" My husband didn't understand why I failed to see the humor in what he had just said. At any rate, I felt I had hit the "feel good" jackpot. If there was one thing I could do and do well, it was make noodles.

My Aunt Gene taught me how to make noodles when I was a little girl. She was a staunch Pentecostal widow who raised five children on her own. I'm not sure when she had time to spend with another child but she did. Her secret to mouthwatering noodles was simple. We would use only fresh farm eggs, make the dough slightly stiff but still pliable, and then roll the dough paper thin with a large homemade rolling pin. Once the large circle of dough dried for a couple of hours, it was tightly rolled to form a long snake-like piece of dough. A sharp knife was necessary to cut the noodles thin; however, I always loved the big doughy, clumped up pieces that stuck together sometimes when they cooked. Only real chicken broth would do, making the aro-ma coming from my Aunt Gene's house on noodle day rival any-thing Chanel or Estee Lauder could produce. Making noodles from scratch is nearly a lost art, as many of today's women choose to take a faster, pre-packaged route.

So, when Frank said he missed his wife's noodles and I knew how to make them, nothing would do but to surprise him for Sunday dinner. My daughter, Elizabeth, was a teenager at that time and I thought it was an opportunity to do some teaching about giving and self-sacrifice for the sheer act of helping an-other human being. She is not especially hands-on like me; in fact she went into Police work, the polar opposite of nursing. But she saw the value in what I was doing and readily agreed to help.

That Sunday we rolled out the pots, pans, and mixing bowls and in no time at all had that familiar aroma of chicken-broth-in-the-making wafting throughout our kitchen. We mixed, kneaded, rolled, and cut noodles. By early afternoon, we were prepared to head to Franks house for a special treat. He knew we were coming and promised to eat light until we arrived.

Once we pulled into his driveway I could see him jump from his chair, grinning very broadly, and race to open his front door. He seemed in better spirits that day than I had previously seen him. I introduced my daughter and told him that even though I was sure the noodles wouldn't even touch his wife's; hopefully they would come in a close second. He was so thankful and ap-preciative that he never stopped smiling.

As we were saying our goodbyes and preparing to leave, I looked at my daughter and to my surprise; the tears were stream-ing down her face. I was very confused by this because we had just had a delightful, positive experience with a very lonely man. I could see by her expression she wanted to get the heck out of there. We had made his day and he was happy, so why wasn't she?

Later she explained to me that she had an unspoken, extraordinary gift. For people less fortunate than her, she had the ability to feel emotion far past empathy. Somehow she could actually physically feel their pain and suffering. In most instances, she didn't walk but ran away from highly emotional experiences.

Her entire life she avoided situations that would tend to pull her from her comfort zone, like the time our beloved family dog, a loveable miniature schnauzer named Poochie, was put down. As much as Elizabeth loved her, it was far easier for her to become busy and simply pretend none of it was happening. Her apparent lack of emotion lead me to believe she didn't care, but quite the opposite was true. The more highly-charged situations became, the more she pulled back.

While the experience with Frank would have been a good way to teach compassion to most teenagers, with her I found it to be unnecessary. The encounter with Frank brought my daughter into light with a newfound respect from me. By keeping her distance, I thought she was unfeeling but it was quite the opposite. I was proud of her and never forced her into that role again.

What I Learned

Anyone who knows me would say that I get my batteries charged by helping people in need. I love to get knee-deep in their misery and fluff until I've done everything I can to make their world better. I'm not sure if I go the extra mile for them or for myself. At any rate, we both benefit and that can't be a bad thing. In spite of this lesson, I still find it difficult to totally understand why some people would rather distance themselves from tough situations rather than roll up their sleeves and get to work. However, I don't know anyone more caring or generous than my daughter, but don't ask her to be "hands on". I've seen her give her last dollar to homeless people, more than once, but that's where her involvement ends. The mere fact that some people are uncomfortable directly serving or caring for the underprivileged, doesn't make them uncaring, thoughtless, or selfish. Some people are thinkers, and some are doers. Come to find out, it takes all kinds to make this big old world go round. We all do our part in our own way.

Denise Plumlee-
Tadlock
2014

Sheila

Sheila was already a Hospice patient by the time I met her. Having her youth stolen by Multiple Sclerosis (MS), she somehow managed to maintain the most positive and cheery attitude. Often being referred to as a "prankster," she loved practical jokes. Her symptoms of MS began early, dating back to age eight; and would be wheelchair-bound by twenty-three. None of this deterred Sheila as she continued to work as an ad designer for our local newspaper, learning to navigate her way around the office in her wheelchair. The newspaper owners, Jack and Bonnie Thatcher, were very instrumental in accommodating Sheila's disability.

Sheila's sister, Connie, told of an experience Sheila once had that would be one of the most "out of control" and frustrating experiences in any person's life. One morning while Sheila and her mom were home, her mom got up to walk to the back of the house and lie down. Instead, she collapsed in the hallway with a massive heart attack. While she was lying there, dying on the floor, Sheila, in her wheelchair, was helpless. Unable to assist in

CPR or even use her hands to call for help, she simply had to sit idly by and watch her mother die. It wasn't until Connie came by later that anyone was aware there was a problem.

I was brought into Sheila's care late in her life. She was very ill; in fact she was dying. Being a former avid shopper, she had been very disappointed that she was unable to go Christmas shopping that year. She had been tethered to her hospital bed in the nursing home, too ill to leave. But her loving sister came up with the most remarkable plan, and together they were able to execute it.

Connie arrived at Sheila's room one cold, snowy winter morning after Christmas and asked if she was ready to go shopping. Sheila happily agreed, and so the plan was set in motion. Connie changed Sheila into some comfortable shopping clothes, put on a bit of make-up, and combed her hair. Connie then pulled her chair as close to Sheila as she could and took her hands. They closed their eyes and took off.

Connie said, "Where do you want to go?" Sheila said that since she was a little tired, maybe just go to a few stores in town.

They went first to the Country Squire and Connie picked out a nice blue dress for Sheila. Sheila said, "You know I don't look good in blue, but what do you think about that blouse hanging on the wall?" It was agreed that Sheila would look pretty in that so they summoned an employee to get it down for them. Sheila also desperately needed a new pair of jeans and after looking at all the latest styles, finally found the perfect pair. An after Christmas sale was in progress so the sisters took full advantage and bought several things. They were quite pleased with the prices and how much they had saved. Once the purchases were made, the girls made their way across the street to a furniture store where Sheila bought a beautiful painting. She thought it would look pretty in her house. They walked up and down each isle noting how comfortable or uncomfortable the different sofas and chairs were.

Both girls were getting hungry by now. An argument ensued between the sisters over where to eat. Connie suggested a nice pizza place, but Sheila informed Connie that she got to choose where to eat last time, so this time it was her turn. Sheila chose Long John Silver's where she ordered chicken. She loved their chicken. Connie had the fish and chips and it was good as well. They sampled each other's food, then laughed at how this was not going to help their waistline. They chuckled too at that darn bell everyone was ringing denoting good service. It was decided that it was a little loud and crowded in there for them so they ate and promptly left.

Satisfied with their purchases and lunch, they decided they'd had enough. Connie drove Sheila home, helped her with her packages, and put her pajamas back on. Sheila was tired but blissful from her shopping trip. She had been confined so long in her nursing home room that she desperately needed a girl's day out, and somehow Connie knew just what to do.

What I Learned

A gift doesn't have to cost a lot, nor does it have to come wrapped in a pretty bow. What Connie did for Sheila couldn't have made her happier. But in order to do what Connie did, you have to think outside the box. What a remarkable journey the girls had that day, and they never left the room. I asked Connie if Sheila walked that day or was she still in her wheelchair. She said emphatically, "Oh she didn't walk, never even thought about it." The wheelchair had become so engrained into who she was that she never even considered walking, even in her fantasy. Sheila died just days after this remarkable outing.

Denise Plumlee-Tadlock
2013

Marilyn

Marilyn was an only child and had never married. She spent her entire adult life lovingly caring for her aging parents. She was a bit backward in nature, timid, and shy. When I first met Marilyn, her mother had already passed. Her entire life was now devoted to her beloved father, Elmo. For many years prior to my involvement with Elmo, he was in steadily declining health. In spite of a few minor medical issues, his decline was largely due to his progression of dementia. His dementia was most likely Alzheimer's, but it was not widely known at that time. Alzheimer's Disease was discovered in 1907, but was not considered a major disease or disorder until the 1970s, just prior to my involvement with him.

I received a phone call from Elmo's doctor asking if we could assist Marilyn in teaching her how to give her newly-diagnosed diabetic father insulin injections. I felt confident in assisting them as I had done it many times in the past. Elmo and Marilyn lived in town in a beautiful brick home. The home was clean and neat as a pin and contained lavish, expensive antiques in every room. Elmo was the antique collector and had been for forty years. I loved going there as I always saw something new (and by that I mean old) each time I went. Much of our time was spent discussing old steam engine tractors as he had both used and collected them.

Marilyn let me know up front that she could not give her father injections. She would do what she could, but not the injections. She said, "Don't ask me, I simply can't." I told her it wasn't that hard, in fact it was easy and we would have this mastered in no time. Elmo, of course, was in no shape to learn how to perform such a detail-oriented task. She was willing to try but remained steadfast in her opinion that she could not stick her father with a needle. I was just as steadfast that she could. I told her I would work with her every day until she felt confident. I understand that just because giving injections comes easy to me, it may not come easy to someone that's not a nurse or of a medical background. I understood that; however, I felt that with enough patience and encouragement I could have gotten even the most stubborn, difficult student to finally reach independence.

For the first few days I simply had Marilyn watch while I performed the entire procedure. I showed her how to roll the insulin bottle, put in equal amounts of air into the bottle and then draw up the ordered units. I demonstrated how to clean the arm, pinch up the skin and stick the needle into the arm. The first several times Marilyn just looked away, confident she could never do it. I started the process very slowly. Her only task at first was to simply get the insulin out of the refrigerator. That's all, just go to the refrigerator and bring it to me. With some reluctance she did. In a few days I had her roll the bottle until the insulin was thoroughly mixed. I always finished the procedure but was happy with our progress, slow as it was.

On the day she was to actually perform the needle stick she continued to state her inability to give her father a shot, or as she called him, Daddy. I said, "Marilyn, you have to. I can't continue to come every day; you don't want to put him in a nursing home, so that just leaves you. You have to do it. Today I will do everything up to the stick, and then you can finish the job. Here, watch me again. You roll the bottle like this, stick the needle in through the rubber cap, draw up 25 units, then take…" BOOM! Down she went. She hit the floor with a thud and scared me to death. I thought, I'll be darned. She can't do it.

I don't think she ever lost consciousness, but she was well on her way. Her skin was clammy and she was white as a ghost. I thought, Boy oh boy, what are we going to do? We seemed to be at an impasse. For the next few days I chose to just do the entire procedure myself and let her have some well-deserved time off. In the meantime, I began checking for any possible solution. The problem seemed to be the actual needle stick. She had already proven that she could draw up the insulin, but that's where she stopped, both mentally and physically.

After many phone calls and hours of research, I found an odd-looking, crude, metal contraption and for the sake of description, I'm going to call it a "syringe hider". I'm sure it had a proper name but I can't recall it now. Once you have your insulin drawn up, you put the syringe in this silver bullet, and close the door. You then can inject the insulin without ever seeing the needle or witnessing the needle going into the skin. I was so excited I ordered one that day and couldn't wait to tell Marilyn about it. She felt it sounded promising too.

It arrived a few days later and I took it with me on my next visit. To this day I can still hear Marilyn giggle as she put the syringe into the "syringe hider" and then do something she never thought possible. She gave Daddy his insulin! She was so proud of herself and I was too. For the two of them, what she'd done was huge. She truly couldn't give him a shot the old fashioned way, and under no circumstances did she want to place him in a nursing home. She felt obligated to care for him until the end, and now she could.

What I Learned

The word commitment is defined as being dedicated to something. Marilyn was committed to her father, and I was committed to Marilyn. I knew somehow we would get this seemingly impossible task accomplished. I didn't know how or when, just that we would. The human spirit is powerful and when someone dedicated is given enough time and patience, nearly anything is possible. Marilyn wanted so badly to help her father, but in order to do so she had to overcome insurmountable fears. Once she became independent, I never had to go back again. She remained, for her father, a solid rock.

Denise Plumlee-Tadlock
2012

Jean

Many years ago I worked with an LPN (licensed practical nurse) at the hospital on the Medical/Surgical unit. I was the 3-11 supervisor and Jean was my midnight replacement. Healthcare was much different "back in the day". Jean was pretty much the only nurse on midnights and the fact that she was not an RN (registered nurse) didn't seem to make any difference. In fact, as far as being responsible, intelligent, and dependable, it didn't matter at all. I would have placed my life in Jean's care any day.

I was always glad to see her face as my shift was finishing. She was staunch and rigid when it came to uniform protocol. Her white uniforms were always clean and very neatly pressed. Her cap sat high and proud on top of her head. Her slightly graying hair gave her the appearance of superiority. I liked Jean and had nothing but the utmost respect for her. She worked circles around a staff half her age and certainly no one could accuse her of being lazy. Even with my college degree, she intimidated me. She was so completely spot on and perfect, I worried that my shift report or performance for that evening might not be up to snuff. I still don't know why I felt that way. She never had an unkind word to me. Maybe I was always fearful of not meeting her standards.

Jean told me a story one evening about her mentally-challenged, adult son who still lived at home with her. Living just on the edge of town, Jean had a few farm animals, including a turkey. This turkey wasn't just any turkey; he was being fattened for a purpose, a glorious Thanksgiving feast. Every day Jean would watch the progress of her turkey and could practically smell the aroma that only an oven baked Thanksgiving Day turkey could give. The day before Thanksgiving, Jean asked her son to go out and kill the turkey so that she could begin the meal preparation. She noticed that he was gone a very long time, and also noticed him pacing nervously back and forth in the backyard. Sometime later he appeared in the house holding a beautiful twenty-pound, ready-to-bake turkey. Jean knew it was twenty pounds because that's what the Butterball tag said. Sure enough, he had walked to town and bought a frozen turkey and handed it to Jean in the familiar yellow plastic netting. He was sure she would be fooled and would never know the difference. Jean said she never did let him know that she knew. Instead, she was angry at herself for asking him to kill what he considered to be the family pet.

About twenty-five years after leaving the hospital, she became one of our home health patients. I was so excited for a chance to get to see her again. I was anxious to reminisce and talk about old times and how we were sure we had it much worse than any generation of nurses before or after us. I wanted to look my best for her. I took extra time with my hair, making sure each and every hair was in place. I took extra care with my makeup too. My eye shadow glowed with a soft summer hue, a few swipes with the rouge brush made my cheeks look alive and healthy, and then I added a bright, summery lipstick to match the mild temperatures. I even bought a colorful set of scrubs to wear. I hate to brag, but I looked good. I anxiously drove to her house that day and stepped on the porch, knowing I was about to blow her away with my still breathtaking good looks. I took a deep breath, straightened out my hair and clothes, and rang the doorbell.

After a few moments Jean opened the door and looked at me, slowly up one side and down the other. Then, she finally spoke. "Well" she said, "I thought Halloween was over." With that she turned and walked back into her house.

And so it was done. Taken out at the knees at such a tender young age. Left speechless. To this day I'm not sure what happened. Was she teasing? Was she demented? Was she serious? I will never know. She did not elaborate nor apologize. All I know is that I drove back to my office that day feeling less than my glorious self.

One of my favorite expression states, "Life is a test. It is only a test. Had this been real life, you would have been instructed where to go and what to do." Perhaps if I had read the handbook, I may have saved myself some uncomfortable humiliation.

What I Learned

Perhaps I didn't mean as much to Jean as she did me, but at any rate I felt a little confused and a lot hurt. I was disappointed until I realized that my big thwarted "ta-da" moment was more about me than about her. I discovered there are reasons it takes all kinds to make up this world. Wouldn't it be a boring and tedious world if we all looked alike, dressed alike, and thought alike? Jean taught me that day to lighten up and not be quite so serious. And yes, we absolutely must learn to laugh at ourselves. It's going to be a long bumpy ride if we don't. And for the record, I did tone things down a bit after that encounter. In all honestly, on that particular day, maybe all I lacked was a rubber ball stuck to my nose.

Denise Plumlee-Tadlude
2014

George

The moments before George died, for most of us, would defy all logic. His last few minutes were both unbelievable and tragic.

George had been a patient of the health department off and on for years. He had been very ill with what the doctor called "farmers lung". He would have far too many bad days, speckled occasionally with a good day. His quality was long gone and he needed assistance for nearly every aspect of his life. Someone had to cook for him, help with his house, and he hadn't driven in years. In his earlier time, he provided a living for his six children (five sons and one daughter) by driving a semi-truck and farming.

George's daughter, Brenda, was one of my nurses' aides. She was one of my most dependable and trustworthy employees. George's son, Curtis, was the maintenance man for the health department. He worked hard and was considered a genuine people-pleaser.

I was sitting at my desk one cold winter afternoon when I

heard Curtis yelling and screaming all over the building. He had gotten a call from his wife, Jessica, and the news was bad. "Help! Help! Can somebody help me? My dad's house is on fire and he's in it! I don't have a car!" Curtis and Jessica shared a car, and she always dropped him off in the morning then went back home until their daughter went to school. The couple lived next door to George, whose house was several miles in the country. Both George and Curtis lived in a mobile home with only a driveway separating the two.

As soon as I heard Curtis' pleas for help, I grabbed my coat and shouted, "Curtis, let's go!" With that, we ran to my car and headed to George. Curtis was nearly inconsolable, not knowing the status of his Dad. When Jessica called, she said George's homemaker was actually in his home the moment the fire started, but couldn't get him out. That all sounded odd. George was ambulatory, mentally sharp, and the homemaker was there when the fire started. How in the world could she not get him out?

George had been on oxygen for years, but he had a bad habit: he liked to smoke. The doctors gave up long ago on getting him to quit, so they did the next best thing. They encouraged him to at least turn his oxygen off when he smoked. Oxygen is very flammable and combustible when it comes in contact with fire. George thought that to be a lot of nonsense and would often light up in spite of the warnings.

Out of nervousness or sheer boredom, he would often play with his cigarette lighter. The lighter was an old flip-top Zippo-type, the kind where you had to shut the lid to get the flame to extinguish. He would sit in his chair and repeatedly light the flame, then shut the lid. Only this time, after the lighter produced a flame, he dropped it. With unbelievable quickness, the fire spread until the entire carpet was on fire. The flame spread almost immediately to his chair, the curtains, and the living room. The homemaker ran to George and pulled on him to get up. He refused. She pulled again but he remained steadfast in his chair. Panic began to set in. Her screams to leave fell onto defiant, deaf ears. George wouldn't get up and time was running out. The fumes were becoming toxic and she knew she had to leave.

Finally, at the last minute, George did get up, but he didn't go toward the door. Instead, with determined intent, he turned and walked slowly down the hall. The homemaker was screaming, "George, this way! Where are you going?" But he knew where he was going. When he reached the end of the hall, he opened the door to his bedroom and peacefully laid down on the bed. By then the smoke was engulfing the home and entry was nearly impossible. With disbelief, the homemaker went out the front door as George went down the hall.

Jessica arrived within a minute or two after the homemaker got outside. Together they made a final attempt to rescue him. They reached for the door and pulled, but it was locked! Locked! How did it get locked? They had no way in. That was when the frantic call to Curtis was made.

I was driving as quickly as I could on the snow-covered roads as Curtis was fearing the worst. As we turned the corner to their shared driveway, we could see black smoke billowing and the entire home was engulfed in flames. At this point we still did not know the outcome; if the homemaker had gotten him out or not. Curtis jumped out of my car while it was still in motion and ran to the house.

They coroner ruled his death an accident, but his family knew better. After years of living in pain, tethered to a confining oxygen tube, and with little quality, George simply saw an opportunity and took it. The fire was not intentional, but his actions following its ignition were.

What I learned

I learned that there can come a time in a person's life when they simply have had enough. To some people, there are things worse than death. While George would have never intentionally harmed himself by setting his house on fire, once it was done, he saw an opportunity that was too strong to resist. The last thing the homemaker saw as she was leaving was the back of George walking slowly down the hall to his room. He knew what would happen. George lay down on his bed and patiently waited to be called home.

Denise Plumber-Tadlock
2012

Mrs. Reverend Earl Phillips

Oh how I wish I could be like the one and only Mrs. Reverend Earl Phillips. When you asked what her name was, that's what she said. I honestly don't even recall what her first name was. My encounter with her was short, but she left a lasting impression. The first time I met her we talked for a few moments and then she did something remarkable. She cupped my face in her hands and said, "Oh, Honey, I love you." And the remarkable thing was I think she did. She had the most angelic qualities of any living creature I have ever met. I believe that she loved everyone and everything. After a spending a short few moments with her, you somehow got the feeling everything was going to be all right. She simply permeated tranquility and a beautiful, peaceful aura.

One day, I needed to draw a blood sample for lab testing. Being able to hit a vein the first time was something that I could do well and prided myself in. The best teacher of all is experience; in fact, I am unaware of anything even remotely close to a comparable substitute. My chest usually puffed up just a little when I was called to assist one of my poor, troubled, younger colleagues who had missed the vein on several occasions and it was time to bring in the "big guns". So, you can imagine my "defeatist, balloon deflating, no wind in my sails attitude" when my luck ran out.

I announced to Mrs. Reverend Earl Phillips that I was going to draw some blood and pulled up a chair to sit close to her. I made small talk as I organized the usual tourniquet, tubes with different colored tops, and needles. I placed the tourniquet around her arm and began to feel for the most useable vein. There it is, found it. I opened the alcohol packet and began the process of "de-germing" the site.

"Hold real still now, you're going to feel a little stick." Hmmm. That's odd. Nothing, not even a flash of blood. With that, I apologized and moved to another spot. I opened another alcohol packet and cleaned where I knew the blood supply was bountiful.

"Here we go again, Mrs. Reverend Earl Phillips. Little stick." I moved the needle around carefully trying to find the blood without causing too much pain to my poor, little, angelic victim. Nada, not even a drop. Starting to feel a little (or perhaps a lot) uncomfortable by now, I apologized profusely and explained to her that I would have to try again. My face was flushed as I squirmed in my seat. My no-fail plan was to move to a different location and carefully choose another spot. Third time's the charm, I reminded myself as I placed the tourniquet this time around her hand. By this time I was wishing the alcohol was of the ingestible kind. Deep breath, careful, careful, easy does it… "What the heck." I choose my frustration words very carefully because after all, my patient was the Mrs. Reverend Earl Phillips. Where is this lady's blood? She's not angelic at all!

I said apologetically, "Mrs. Reverend Earl Phillips, I am so sorry. This never happens to me. If you trust me, I will hunt for another place to try."

With that she said something that seemed so utterly simplistic. "If you would like, you can take my blood here," she suggested as she pointed to some obscure place on her arm. "No one has been able to get blood from those veins in ten years."

I did indeed try "there" and immediately got three vials of beautiful, bright-red blood. The problem was she trusted me and my knowledge explicitly and never felt it necessary to tell me where she kept her secret supply of veins. All that time, all I had to do was ask.

What I Learned

While playing outside one summer afternoon, a little boy found a lost, wondering snapping turtle. Knowing that snapping turtles, or snappers, live in water and this turtle was nearly a mile from the pond, he felt he had to risk being bitten in order to return the snapper to water. It was hot and the turtle was heavy, but the little boy was proud of his accomplishment as he placed the turtle back in the pond. When he arrived home he happily told his mother what he'd done. Much to the little boy's surprise, his mother told him that even though she was proud of him for doing what he thought was right, in reality what he did was probably harmful to the turtle.

She explained that snappers will often travel long distances to reach sandy soil to lay eggs. That turtle probably spent several days or weeks crawling through the field to lay her eggs, and he had just put her back in the pond. While this lesson may have been sad for the little boy to learn, the moral of the story is important: ask the turtle first. As individuals we know our bodies better than anyone. I never attempt to obtain a blood sample now before first asking, "Do you have a place that's better than another for getting blood?" Twelve words. I ask every time now. It seems to save a lot of time and pain. Always ask the turtle first.

Neva

Webster defines determination as, "A fixed movement toward an object or end, firmness of purpose, a fixed intention or resolution, fortitude, perseverance, and conviction." Each and every one of those words describes Neva.

Neva was another of my very first home health patients. As a young nurse, I badly wanted to get into my patients' lives and fix each and every one of their problems, but that's usually where the trouble started. A problem to me was not necessarily a problem to them.

Neva was crippled with rheumatoid arthritis, or RA as it's known. For those of you who may not be familiar with RA, here is a general synopsis. Rheumatoid arthritis is a chronic inflammatory disorder that typically affects the small joints in hands and feet. Unlike the wear-and-tear damage of osteoarthritis, rheumatoid arthritis affects the lining of your joints, causing a painful swelling that can eventually result in bone erosion and joint deformity. I'm sure many of you have seen people with their fingers twisted and bent into a painful looking unusable configuration. That's RA. Many times if the patient lives long enough, they eventually become wheelchair bound. This is the point in Neva's where we first met.

Neva lived far out in the country, far away from family, medical care, shopping, or any of the things we would find necessary. She lived with her parents until their death and then inherited the old, rundown, family farmhouse. She had never been married, so for a large part of her life she relied solely on herself. That is well and good up to a point, but then logic should overtake our thinking and allow us to make better decisions, or at least what I considered better.

Starting with my first visit to Neva, and each and every one thereafter, I talked to her about moving to town. I assured her that she would have everything she would need to allow her to stay home: close supervision, safety, home delivered meals, doctors, hospital, stores, and a social life. She was lacking in all of those things. I would lecture her about how unsafe it was for her to be living this far out in the country. Of course back then, there was no button to wear around your neck to summon help in case of an emergency. Neva would smile sweetly, thank me for my concern, and state how she was exactly where she wanted to be. After living there her entire life, moving was not something she was prepared to do.

As usual, after my visit and before I left she would always ask me to do something for her. She had her entire day's menu decided and would have me open her cabinets and set the food on the counter. I poured cereal in a bowl and milk from the gallon container into a small cup with handle or open a can of soup and put it in the pan on the stove. I opened cans of tuna and boxes of crackers or set out some bread. Before I left, her countertop contained that day's entire food intake, all neatly arranged by meals and ready to eat. All she had to do was wheel herself into the kitchen and prepare it. In addition to my visits, she also had a homemaker that worked two or three times a week. The home-maker would set the meals on the counter the same as me, and wash whatever dishes there were to wash.

Concern for Neva and her being unable to care for herself troubled me. Each and every visit I said to her, "Neva, you have to move to town. It isn't safe here and you can't live this way." She would smile sweetly, ignore my pleas, and ask if I would please open this or that and set it on the counter. I told her each and every time how she needed to move. In fact, I told her every time until her death, at home, three years later. Do I need to review what the word "determination" means?

She had no intentions of moving, ever. By simply smiling and being non-combative, she managed to keep everyone on her side and doing what it took to keep her exactly where she wanted to be, home. I still can't believe she did that. And I admire her for it.

What I Learned

When you look at what the human spirit can achieve, it's truly unbelievable. Neva exemplified everything that is possible when we simply put our minds to it. Once I saw a poster that said, "First, decide what it is you want. Then, do what you have to do to achieve it." Neva must have seen that poster. There was no backing down, no meeting halfway, no compromise. Neva knew what she wanted and what she had to do to achieve it. Truly, the human spirit is the strongest and most powerful tool in the world.

Denise Humes-Tadlock
2018

Gerald

Occasionally the health department would get a phone call, usually anonymous, requesting us to do a welfare check on someone. Most of the calls came from neighbors who were, for the most part, well-meaning. The usual nature of the call was almost always along the lines of self-neglect. The caller would declare, "They need help. The health department has to do something." We would always go and then referrals to assisting agencies were made, but rarely was any type of action forced. The following story is a welfare check I conducted on an elderly man years ago.

Gerald moved to the country after living his whole life in St. Louis and working for the government. He yearned to reside in rural America and live as country folks do. One of his first purchases when he left the city was a group of hybrid goats. He was proud of his goats and had them for decades. Gerald began to neglect his farm, both the inside and out. Entire summers would go by without ever mowing his yard. No maintenance or upkeep to his house had occurred in years. At one point, his bathroom window fell out, casing and all. The inside was nearly beyond description. His general health was in the same state as his home, given that he didn't trust doctors and hadn't left his home in thirty-five years. Let me repeat that because it warrants it. He had not been off his property in thirty-five years. Even so, no one bothered this aging, eccentric old man until the day he made a phone call to the sheriff's department.

Gerald wanted to report some unruly, young boys. They had been coming by his property late at night and doing unspeakable things to his goats. Whether this was true or not, only the goats know. But that phone call initiated a referral to senior services, which in turn initiated a referral to the health department for a medical welfare check. Gerald was clearly in need of medical, social, and financial care, but we didn't know where to start. When you have a case that is so complex, you have to break it down piece by piece and look at the most critical things first, which is food and nutrition.

Bad things can happen when you haven't seen a doctor for over thirty years. He had untreated cataracts so he was left completely blind. His eyes were glossed over with a white milky hue which gave him the appearance of an alien. In order to keep track of his food during the day, he would place what he was going to eat in a lunch bucket which he chained to his ankle. Lost food was no longer a problem. What he usually ate was potatoes that he would cook in the crudest of fashions. He would put a Dutch oven on top of a hot plate and bake potatoes. He would wash them down with a nice glass of salt water. To keep the coons that dwelled inside his home out of his other food such as eggs and raw potatoes, he would place the items inside a metal trash can in his living room and secured it with a heavy chain.

Neglected health care was next on the list to assess. His cataracts were far too gone to remedy, but something needed to be done about his feet and toes. Gerald had a bad case of fungus on his feet from continually wearing rubber boots. He had to wear the boots because at night the rats would gnaw and chew on his toes and that was his only way of keeping the rodents away. In addition to staving off the rats, the boots also helped to prevent sores on his ankle from the strapped lunch bucket.

Gerald's family was as involved as he would allow them to be. We would occasionally phone one of his two children and tell them he was in dire straits and needed help. They would come right down but he would not allow them to enter his home. In fact, he kept a bale of straw inside his back door to prevent passage. When in town, they were required to stay at one of the local motels. Not that they would have been able to stay in his home even if he'd wanted them to.

When I went on my first welfare check to Gerald, it became dangerously close to being my last. Gerald didn't like me, not one bit. By the time I began my investigation, he'd had enough of people stopping by and telling him what he needed to do for his own good. There were excrement piles on his sofa that I have no doubt belonged to him. He didn't trust me and wanted to be left alone. When I pushed a little too far for him to go to a nursing home, he simply reached beside him and placed his shotgun on his lap. End of conversation. It didn't take me long to get back to my car.

Gerald was eventually declared incompetent and forcefully removed from his home. An interesting detail was that on the day he was removed, he passed what is called a mini-mental. A mini-mental is a brief, standardized 30-point questionnaire test that is used to screen for cognitive impairment. Typically if one can pass a mini-mental, then they are untouchable. But in this case, a physician and judge declared him incompetent even though he passed the test, and he was immediately removed from his home. The evidence of self-neglect was too overwhelming to ignore. As he was being taken away, he looked at his case-worker, one of the few people he trusted, and said "You were supposed to be my friend. You have deceived me." Gerald died three years later in the nursing home from pneumonia.

What I Learned

Abraham Lincoln, one of the greatest politicians of our time, was quoted as saying "When I do good, I feel good. When I do bad, I feel bad. That is my religion." Isn't that simple, straight forward, and true? But come to find out, it isn't always true, and with Gerald, it certainly wasn't. We did our research and homework, and as hard as it was, we knew what he needed and what had to be done. But instead of being left with a warm, fuzzy feeling because we did good, we all felt terrible. I recall one of my nursing instructors in 1973 telling me to never let my age or modesty prevent me from taking charge when it was my responsibility to do so. I hope Gerald eventually forgave me.

Russell and Ruth Ann

Make no mistake about it, I loved my job. Home Health is a completely different type of nursing than in any other job I've ever experienced. In my medical career, I have worked in a hospital, doctors office, nursing home, emergency room, and performed insurance physicals. While all facets of nursing are worthwhile, some are just more arduous or mentally exhausting than others. Nothing, however, even comes remotely close to home health for me as far as satisfying employment. As patients, they are no longer under the microscope or rule of someone or someplace else. Also, they no longer have to do what we ask them to do because, contrary to a hospital or institutional setting, we are in their home and they have the upper hand. All they have to do is ask us to leave and it's over. But on the plus side, we get to know our patients on a much more personal level and in some ways, they do us. Come to find out though, that's not always a good thing.

I had been making visits to Russell for a couple of months and he and his wife, Ruth Ann, were delightful. Once while visiting, Russell reflected on how he met Ruth Ann. He originally hailed from Oklahoma, but migrated to Clay County during the 1939 oil boom. One evening he and a buddy decided to drive to town and "have a cool one." When they arrived, it just so happened that his buddy's girlfriend was walking along the sidewalk with one of her friends. Her name was Ruth Ann. Russell recalled her being tall, slim, and as pretty as a picture. He remarked that the thing that drew him to her was her hat. He stated he fell in love with her on that first encounter because of her hat. It made her look so polished, so sophisticated. Russell stared off into the distance for a while and then finally remarked, "I don't believe she's worn a hat since."

Russell had a bad heart and required close supervision of his vital signs and medication to make sure he had the right combination of treatment. They always listened intently when I spoke and gave instructions as they wanted to do everything correctly in order to ensure he remained as healthy as possible. The two were nearly an ideal home health experience. Much of the time all of our instruction and teaching with our patients is forgotten as soon as we walk out the door, but they tried, they really tried.

Russell and Ruth Ann delighted in hearing about my two children. They were childless themselves, so hearing about Christmas programs, piano recitals, ballgames, and birthday parties pleased them. Over several weeks we became very close and we all looked forward to each visit. After the mandatory medical assessment and paperwork, we would spend quite some time catching up on our personal lives. They would tell me about this niece or that relative, and I would regale with whatever was the current event in my life. They were always anxious to hear the follow-up to a story from the week before. How did your cake turn out? Did you get your garden planted? Did your daughter pass her math test? Nice, cozy, sweet…wrong.

I normally made my visit to them each Wednesday morning, but for some reason the stress level at work had hit an all-time high that week and I desperately needed a mental health day. So, I called in sick on Wednesday and had the secretary call my appointments for the day and tell them I wouldn't be there. The following day I went to Russell and Ruth Ann's first as I was anxious to tell them about my near burn-out experience. They were like grandparents. I thought they would hug me and tell me it was all going to be okay. Ruth Ann would tell me to sit down while she poured me a cup of coffee and immediately get to fixing me a hearty breakfast. That's what people do when someone they care about is hurting.

As usual, I walked into their house armed with my customary bag of blood pressure and heart monitoring paraphernalia. We both said good morning and then I apologized for being absent the day before. I told them I had really been under a lot of stress and needed a day off.

Ruth Ann turned to me and with fire in her eyes and with a raised voice said, "And what do you do with your patients when you need a day off? Just abandon them?" With that she threw a dish towel and walked out of the room. Wow. I was both blindsided and sucker-punched in the same powerful blow. I'm sure you've heard of people in a near-death experience feeling they looked upon the face of God? Well, in that flash of anger I'm pretty sure I looked upon the face of Lucifer. I thought we were friends. I thought she cared about me and I was hurt. In reality, it appeared she only cared about me when it was convenient for her. We were never the same again. In fact, I was never the same again. Never did I open my personal life to anyone or share more than just the usual superficial small talk again. I really hated that, but it was my fault. I stepped way outside my professional boundaries in caring for this couple and paid for it dearly. We remained cordial but our relationship was strained from that moment on.

What I Learned

While this story contains nearly all the elements for a good book or romance: respect, betrayal, anger, joy, and hurt, none of those things belong in a professional patient-caregiver relationship. I learned my lesson and I learned it well. I think I knew not to cross that line all along, but I simply liked Russell and Ruth Ann. As creatures with feelings, we have a tendency to simply forget and occasionally let our guards down; after all, we're only human. Even so, being human also gives us the ability to separate our personal life from our professional life. I'd highly suggest you treat your clients or patients with courtesy and respect, but remain aware of the boundary line. It just might prevent having a dish towel thrown at you.

Larry

Larry was one of my first really complicated wound-care cases that I encountered as a young traveling nurse. He had been in a serious motorcycle accident and received a severe fracture of his right femur. About two inches from the bend of his groin, he had a six-inch open incision, or wound. The top of this thigh revealed something, at least for me, never before seen. There, in plain sight, was his thigh bone. The wound was deep, nasty, and scared me to death. My task was to perform what was known as a wet-to-dry dressing daily. The moisture from the impregnated gauze was to prevent the tissue from drying out and assist in healing.

Larry lived off the beaten path in an old model single-wide mobile home. I recall it being summertime as the heat was sweltering. The front yard was brown and free from grass, mostly due to several big unchained dogs running loose.

Nice looking, pleasant, and approximately my age is how I would most accurately describe Larry. He met me at the door walking on crutches as his doctor ordered no weight bearing on his broken leg for several weeks. I introduced myself and explained that I was there to change the bandage on his leg and asked where would be the best place. He said the sofa in the living room would work best as the light was better and getting to the wound easiest there. He carefully lowered his body to the couch, his right leg being closest to me. I knelt beside him and spread my supplies on a sterile towel on the floor.

I know that I was, and still am, a bit naïve, but what he did next was shocking to me. Or at the least it made me pause, become uncomfortable and remain uncomfortable for the remainder of the time I cared for him. His incision was about two inches down from the bend in his groin, directly across from what one would consider "extreme personal space." For my convenience, he thoughtfully folded his boxers above the wound so I would have easy access. No problem. I then assembled my supplies for use and donned my gloves. As I turned around to start the process, he had quietly placed an open Playboy magazine just above his wound. He said, "You don't mind if I read while you do that, do you?" I said I guess not and he relayed to me that he did not look at Playboy just for the pictures, that he found the articles of great interest. He continued to look at the magazine flipping through page after page while I sweated it out. I finished my wet-to-dry dressing, gathered my supplies and ran from the house.

I don't mind telling you, the next day and the next; in fact all the time until he was discharged, I dreaded going there. I was uncomfortable and uneasy. In all honesty, he was pleasant, and actually a very sweet fellow. Never once did he say anything out of line, but something always made my stomach churn as I was turning into his drive. In retrospect, I wonder why I allowed myself to be put in such an uncomfortable place. I have never been especially assertive and being that way can cripple a person if the issue is left unchecked. Any issue, when you are put in a place of feeling uncomfortable and it is not addressed, will most likely not resolve itself.

What I Learned

Part of the lesson with Larry simply comes from growing up. I was very young, and usually with age comes wisdom. Being quiet, shy, and unassertive only works in certain situations. I have found that in this big ol' world, when it comes right down to it, no one looks out for you but you. I don't mean that I don't have people that love me and look out for my wellbeing, but for the most part, I am responsible for my own safety. No one, and I repeat no one, would ever put me in such an uncomfortable place now. We would come to an understanding and it would be swift and it would be immediate. It isn't always necessary to be blunt or rude either, just make your statement, and then if changes don't occur, it's okay to kick it up a notch. I should have never spent my entire summer dreading that visit. Initially if I had just come to an understanding with him, look at how much more pleasant things would have gone for me.

Randy

Even when you think you may have encountered every possible home visit scenario, be it for the good or bad, there is always room to be surprised. Randy was one of the nicest gentlemen I had ever met. He was in his eighties, still spry for his age, and distinguished looking. He had beautiful gray hair and tanned skin, and looked a lot like Bob Barker from The Price is Right. Unfortunately, aging often steals a portion of our former selves. I truly believe that as our senses begin to deteriorate, (hearing, vision, ability to smell and taste) so do the habits and trademarks that made us who we once were. My grandma is a good example of this. Always neat and pristine, she would get ready for church in the dirtiest blouse or dress. I didn't understand why she would do that, but I do now. Her senses were dulled and she was simply unaware of the small detail that negatively affected her life.

The same was true with Randy. You just got the feeling he had been something at one time. He not only dressed differently, he just looked different. He was from Chicago, being transferred late in life due to his business. He grew to like Flora and decided to retire here. Anyone who has lived in Clay County would know "he's not from around here." He had been a successful business man at one time, and that's why his disheveled home and appearance confused me.

The reason I was seeing him was due to his severe chronic obstructive pulmonary disease, or COPD. He was on oxygen constantly, and the simple act of breathing was difficult. That's why I tried to get him to adopt out his little yappy dogs. There were at least three or four, and often Randy let days go by without letting them out. The stench from inside the house was toxic. The nurses who cared for him would often have to make some excuse to go outside just to breathe fresh air. With his COPD, the dogs made it a horrible environment for him to breathe and live in. This is where the sensory problems exhibited themselves. I know he had no idea how bad his living environment had gotten. On most days you could smell his house from his driveway. He wasn't like that in his younger days, and he wouldn't have lived like that even in his eighties if he was simply aware. Perhaps there was some early dementia surfacing but at any rate, and in spite of everything, I liked him.

I was the one who went on Randy's first visit and performed his admission into home health. He lived in a small, old trailer in town. I found his house easy enough and went to the front door and knocked. Randy came to the door smiling, wearing his oxygen…and a black Speedo. That was all. And he was tanned, all over. I thought, Well, this is different. Seems like a nice enough fella though." He smiled warmly and invited me into his home.

We went into his house and I set up my workstation to begin my assessment. I was unsure about some of his medication and had some questions. He stated he didn't mess with his medicine but he shouted to the back of the house, "Can you come out here and show this nice lady what you do with my medicine?" From the back of the house emerged Merle, also wearing a Speedo. Merle was ninety. I was getting an uneasy feeling about this pair. I was somewhat uncomfortable because, even though I wasn't 100% positive, I was pretty sure they were gay. This young naive nurse from Clay County had no experience with the "likes of them", and I am sorry to admit that in Clay County back in the 80s that was not a very accepted lifestyle. I didn't know what to do with a gay patient. Did being gay make them dangerous? Were they bad people or lazy or perhaps high strung? They didn't have two heads nor were small children unsafe around them. Randy did admit to our social worker a few weeks later that they were gay and had been a couple for decades. I found out they were just like every other couple that I took care of. They were funny. They lived and loved like everybody else. What a horrible, incorrect stereotype ill-informed people have of gay couples. I truly enjoyed them, but I would be remiss if I didn't acknowledge I had some discomfort for a while. The men in my life would never wear a Speedo, but then again, maybe they should.

What I Learned

More than anything, I think Randy and Merle forced me to grow up. My view on the world needed expanding badly, and they help me do that. Until the day I met Randy, I honestly don't think I had ever been outside of Illinois, other than my short stint in Michigan. Most certainly, my circle of family and friends never exposed me to anything other than the jeans wearing, diesel truck driving, sports driven men that I had been used to my entire life. I am grateful to Randy and Merle. I am glad our paths crossed. They taught me to broaden my thinking, and my heart. I learned to care for everyone equally, regardless of sexual orientation. I don't know what happened to Randy's Speedo when he passed on, but if I thought they might have fit my husband, they may have found a new home.

Denise Plumlee—Tadlock
2013

Darlene

Country music legend Barbara Mandrel had a number one hit that went "I was country, when country wasn't cool." Well, Darlene was hoarding, when hoarding wasn't cool. She undoubtedly both invented and perfected it. Hoarding is acquiring and failing to throw out a large number of items that would appear to have little or no value to others (e.g., papers, notes, flyers, newspapers, clothes). Eventually it will cause severe cluttering in the home and it will no longer be a viable living space

At least twenty-five years ago, a phone call came in late one afternoon from Darlene. She wasn't especially shook up or excited. She said, "Could someone come out and check on my husband? I don't think he's okay." I asked what she meant. She replied, "I just think there's something terribly wrong."

Sensing what she wasn't saying, I asked, "Darlene is he breathing?" and she said she didn't think so. I told her I would be right there. I grabbed my bag of medical supplies and took off to her house. She only lived a few blocks away so I could be there in minutes. This was before the 911 emergency services, so it was just considered a welfare check.

When I arrived the lawn was surprisingly manicured. There was a winding sidewalk and little concrete angel ornaments sitting along the path. I thought, What a quaint, cute little home. When Darlene answered the door, it took her a while to push it open far enough so that I could enter. Once inside, I got the feeling I had entered another world, a world much different from my own. There must have been thousands of newspapers stacked everywhere. They were stacked from floor to ceiling in at least a dozen rows. They had an older model wood stove and there was enough fire wood in the living room to last a couple of months. I have no idea how the house had not caught fire by now, but it was an accident waiting to happen. I was in a cluttered labyrinth and I'm sure my eyes were big as quarters. There were books, boxes, clothes, and shoes. There were piles and piles as far as the eye could see.

There was a tiny path that led to the kitchen where I encountered more piles and piles of who knows what. Several 6-8 foot stacks of old Styrofoam meal containers filled the kitchen, as well as dishes, pots, pans, food, hundreds of cool whip and butter tubs, and full trash cans. There was probably a table somewhere, but I'm not sure. By now, you probably have a pretty good mental picture of her house.

Darlene was very glad when I arrived and was rightfully focused on her husband. She said, "Come quickly. He's in the bedroom." We wove through another maze of items Darlene deemed far too important to discard. She opened an interior door and we walked into the bedroom together. She was obviously anxious for me to make my assessment and determine the extent of his condition.

I swear to you, what I said next is neither an exaggeration, nor is it untrue. I stood about 5 feet inside the bedroom and asked, "Darlene, where is he?"

She said, "Right there." " We were standing inside a small, square room, and I couldn't find him. After some pointing and nudging, I eventually saw a foot sticking out from behind some piles. I quickly darted between the narrow paths that led me to her husband. Sure enough, he wasn't alright. He hadn't died yet, but he had suffered a stroke, was dehydrated and his temperature was higher than my thermometer would register. I called the ambulance but wondered how in the world they would get him out.

I wondered if they do what the rock stars do when they have a concert with thousands of people. At some point in a song they throw themselves off the stage into the raised arms of their fans. The fans then pass the body from front to back, or "crowd surf". I was pretty sure that wouldn't be the method of removal, but then again, I had no other options. The ambulance crew did manage to get him out and take him to the hospital where he died the next day.

Several referrals for Darlene were made over the next few weeks, mostly regarding the condition of her living standards. A list of homemakers was given to her to privately pay for assistance, but it was refused. I notified Senior Services, where a "free" homemaker was offered, then declined. She did not see the problem, nor the point of all the fuss. She was happy and content living as she had for many years. She saw no purpose in changing now, and didn't.

What I Learned

There are lots of clichés that could be used in this particular scenario such as:

- *Waste not want not*

- *Different strokes for different folks*

- *It takes all kinds*

- *One man's trash is another man's treasure*

  In a world where we would love to change everyone to fit our standard, it is not always possible or right. Darlene had lived that way her entire life. If I was to remove her from her home and place her in a beautiful upscale neighborhood in an expensive house, within months it would most likely look just like the one described. We have seen it happen time and time again. You can offer help, but more times than not it is rejected. At that point I have my own cliché.

- *You can't change a leopard's spots. They are who they are. Work with your patients, families, or friends on their level instead of trying to make them into something they are not, and the results will be far more successful.*

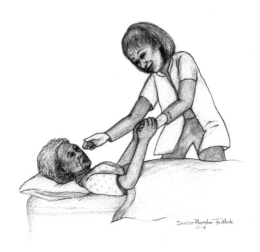

Helen

The incident with this patient may have been the most influential turning point in my nursing career. I remember it like it was yesterday. This story is not going to put me in a good light, or paint a pretty picture of me, but it is what it is. You must remember my point throughout this entire book is how my patients made me a better person due to their influence, even if they were unaware. This was certainly true with Helen.

I had asked the Health Department for years to grant us Good Friday as a paid holiday. My wanting the holiday didn't really have as much to do with the religious ramifications as it did with my own personal desires. The Health Department only allowed a few precious paid holidays, and Good Friday wasn't one of them. If you look on a calendar, there is a long stretch between the clustered holidays of Thanksgiving, Christmas, and New Year's Day and the next one. After requesting for years to receive Good Friday off, in 1989 my efforts finally paid off. For the first time we had a wonderful, well deserved, paid, 3-day weekend between New Year's Day and the 4th of July.

As my luck would have it, the on-call rotation fell so that I was on call for Good Friday weekend. I couldn't believe it; I mean what were the odds? I was the one who fought to get it and I was the one who had to work. Oh well, I would only have to work if there was an afterhours call or some type of emergency. And by the end of the week, it looked like some perfect weather, family time, and nothing to do but whatever I wanted was well within my grasp.

My husband and I had an exciting weekend planned with our four-year-old son and eight-year-old daughter. We were going to color Easter eggs the old- fashioned way. We boiled the eggs and then dipped them into the only egg coloring product available at the time. There was a variety of colors: red, blue, green, yellow, and whatever the color turned when you dipped one egg into all of the colors. My kids thought they were quite the hellions to disregard the box instructions by mixing colors and then laugh at their sinister ways. They felt sure they were outlaws like James Dean or Jessie James. That thin aluminum or metal wire dipper was a device more for getting parents frustrated than dipping eggs, but it was the only gadget available at the time. The entire process was so much fun. I looked forward to it every year and this year was especially great, I had a three-day weekend.

As work day on Thursday was ending, I was in the best mood: a new paid holiday, three days off, springtime, and Easter with my family. I couldn't wait to get the ball rolling. Then at 4:30, just as I was getting ready to leave, the phone rang. It was the Salem Hospital calling about a referral for home health. Not only did the patient need to be seen daily over the next three days, they needed to be seen that evening. I was beyond furious. This was the worst case scenario for me. I remember sitting down at my desk and crying. The wonderful weekend that I was going to spend with my family decorating Easter eggs and doing whatever I wanted was gone. And I was angry; tight fisted, teeth clenched, hard breathing angry.

Helen had colon cancer and had received surgery to remove a large blockage that was preventing her from eating. The blockage was nearly complete and everything she ate eventually came up. The colon needed to rest and heal, so a colostomy was performed. A colostomy is where the colon is cut and the end is brought out through the side of the abdomen. A bag is worn for the sake of catching the bowel contents, or stool. To most people, a colostomy is a very disfiguring and degrading procedure to have. Now couple the disfiguring procedure with being seventy-five years old, scared, confused, and a having new cancer diagnosis with a very poor prognosis. Helen's days of being a wife, mother, and grandmother seemed numbered.

New colostomy's can be complicated and tricky, so hours of teaching and education had to take place. Helen was very frail, very ill, and completely uninformed about how to care for her newly disfigured body. There had already been accidents from a popped bag that ended in bowel leakage all over her clothing. From my desk that Thursday afternoon, I simply didn't care. I was only concerned about me, my family, and how she so terribly inconvenienced me. Under duress, I collected myself, gathered my medical supplies, and took off for her house.

Helen was a tiny lady who was very frightened and was in a terribly disheveled state. Her colostomy bag was off and she couldn't get it back on or to stay in place. She was in pain and knew that she was dying. When I walked into her bedroom, she grabbed my hand, looked at me with begging eyes, and asked so softly and so sweetly for help. She continued to squeeze my hand, thanked me over and over for coming, and remarked that I must surely be an angel.

Here was a woman who had not only undergone a disfiguring surgery but was also given a death sentence, and all I could think about was how she ruined my weekend of Easter egg coloring. Immediately, or sooner if there is something faster than immediately, my attitude changed and my anger subsided. How thoughtless and self-centered was I? How in the world did I get so callous, so unfeeling? Whatever the case, in those first few moments after my arrival, she changed me forever.

Life at the Tackitts' continued and we ended up having a wonderful Easter weekend. We got the eggs colored, hidden, and hunted. We made a bunny cake that in no way resembled a bunny. Without a doubt, Helen brought me full circle and reminded me of why I became a nurse. I have never been so ashamed or so humbled by any other occasion in my life. There can be time for work, and still be time for family. My family wanted me, but my patient needed me. It all worked out and I became a better person.

What I Learned

Each day we are given an opportunity to make the most of what we can with our available time. Some days we will simply have more than others. There will only be one first step taken, one first Christmas, perhaps only one championship game or school play. In spite of wanting to never miss a single event with our families, when we make a commitment to our job, to our patients, then that's what it should be. They need us. Sometimes, just as much as our families do. There will be time for everything. Occasionally we may need to take a step back and breathe deeply, but things will work out, they always do. And Helen, I am so sorry that I put myself before you. You were the true angel.

Denise Plumlee-Tadlock

Lillian

Sometimes in life we do what we think is right, only to find out it wasn't. Such is the case with Lillian and her family. Lillian was an adorable elderly lady with the sweetest disposition. Her husband had been gone for many years and for the most part, Lillian did very well on her own. She was fortunate that she had a strong, supportive family, something that seems to be a precious commodity these days. Her three children all lived close and checked on her daily. They kept her lawn mowed, groceries in the house, and took her to her doctor appointments. They were a wonderful extension to my care. Clearly, they loved their mother.

Lillian began displaying symptoms of chest and lung problems, including shortness of breath and an irritating cough that just wouldn't go away. After determining that it wasn't just a bad chest cold, her doctor ordered a lung x-ray. Sure enough, there was cancer present in both lungs. You might have thought this would be a devastating diagnosis for this elderly lady, but not so. The reason for her nonchalant attitude and being unconcerned is not what you might expect. Her family chose to keep the diagnosis a secret from her. In doing what they thought was right, they also commissioned her doctor to be a party to their well thought out plan. Remember, this was many years ago before HIPPA or strong patient rights. The family chose to opt out of treatment due to her advanced age and poor prognosis.

Once the diagnosis was made and the plan to go home and rest was decided, that's what was done. Lillian went home thinking she just had a bout of bronchitis and that she was well on her way to recovery. And in all honesty, it did work pretty well for her. For the most part she felt good and went about her day happy and content.

On her discharge from the hospital, due to the nature of her illness, Home Health was ordered. I had been told by her doctor and the hospital personnel to not disclose her diagnoses. She did not know she had cancer and her family wanted that information kept form her. I didn't agree with this but I played along as well. It certainly wasn't my place to interfere.

Upon my arrival on a home visit a few weeks into her care, I immediately sensed a change in her. I performed my assessment and went through the usual routine. As I was preparing to leave, she asked if she could show me something. I said, "Of course," not knowing what it was.

She said, "Look at the bill I got from the hospital today. Under the diagnosis it says 'carcinoma, bilateral lung.' Doesn't that mean cancer? Do I have cancer of both lungs?"

I don't know if what I did next was right or wrong, but I wasn't about to look that beautiful, intelligent woman in the eye and tell a complete lie. I said, "Yes, Lillian, that's what it means. Carcinoma, bilateral lung means cancer in both lungs."

The look on her face was of pure devastation. Her devastation was not in the diagnosis, but in the deceit. She couldn't believe that everyone was in on the plot; her doctor, her family, and me.

The only reason I feel the withholding of information, the secrecy, was a forgivable offense is because I know in her children's hearts they loved their mother and thought they were protecting her. They wanted to spare her any undo grief but by doing so, they created a horrible atmosphere of distrust, anger, and resentment.

Lillian and her family did eventually patch things up, as I knew they would, but not without some cutting scars. She felt very out of control of her fate and thought that she might even had chosen treatment. At any rate, she died about a year later in the arms of her very loving family.

What I Learned

I'm sure everyone reading this book is familiar with the expression "Honesty is the best policy". Come to find out it almost always is. Human beings are not as fragile as we think they are. I have always heard it said that people will never ask a question in which they are not prepared to hear the answer. This was true with Lillian. She asked the doctor point blank in the hospital if she had cancer and was told she did not. She was prepared at that moment to hear the truth. Even so, I don't think we should be too hard on her family. They made their decision based on love and the overwhelming need to protect her. And honestly, (trust me from experience when I say this) we could use a lot more children like them.

Denise Plumlee-Tadlock
3-d-13

Emma

I thought for a long time before including this chapter in my book. Its significance is embarrassingly small, yet the message impacted me for 25-30 years. In fact, a week hasn't passed without what I learned finding its way back into the guilt receptors of my brain. As silly, mundane, and trite as this story may seem, I somehow had to find a way for its inclusion.

Emma came from a large family with lots of brothers and sisters. She said that's probably why she had a large family herself with four boys and four girls. Both Emma and her husband were strong, active church members. The children were practically raised in their church, and all eight children felt the members of their small country church were family also. Some of her children drifted geographically away and some never ventured far, but all of them remained very strong in their faith and they themselves became pillars of their respective churches.

One afternoon as I was visiting Emma, I had an occasion to meet her daughter, Lynn. Lynn and her family had traveled from Wisconsin to spend time with Emma on her birthday. The previous summer, Lynn had a once in a lifetime opportunity of fulfilling a lifelong dream. She was selected to participate in her church's mission work in a terribly underprivileged part of our world, Guatemala. Being a nurse, the mission included not only building a school and a church, but also to help deliver some much needed medical care. The level of curable disease caused from infestation such as worms and lice was staggering.

Lynn was open in her experience and loved to talk about the people and how warm and receptive they were to their presence. One of the things that stood out to me the most was something she just happened to mention in a passing thought.

Lynn learned that one of the many things she took for granted in the United States was our endless supply of running water. She lavished herself each day in long, hot showers. The toilet seemed to flush constantly, and it was nothing to turn on the tap and let the water run for several minutes while the water lowered to a cooler drinking temperature. She said that each day in Guatemala, she was allowed only a small bowl of water. With that scant amount she was expected to bathe, shampoo, and brush her teeth.

Immediately she was humbled and realized that water was a precious commodity, and how we take it for granted. Before her trip to Guatemala, Lynn would turn on the faucet and let the water run the whole time she was brushing her teeth. Suddenly, what was second nature seemed so wasteful.

And wouldn't you know it, nearly every time I turn on the faucet now to brush my teeth, when I leave the water running I think of how wasteful I am. Do I think about it every time? Maybe not every time, but often enough in the last thirty years. Have I changed my ways as a result of our conversation? I would love to admit that I have, but I am spoiled. Even though I am wrought with guilt, I never really altered my process.

What I Learned

I learned that I have a guilty conscious when doing something that I know is wasteful and wrong. I learned that breaking old habits is nearly impossible. I learned that as an American I am spoiled, assuming, and expectant. Yet, knowing all those things I continue to let the water run while I brush my teeth. I guess I also learned that I'm only human and not perfect.

Denise Plumlee-Tadlock

Mildred

Without a doubt, Mildred was one of my favorite patients. She was very elderly and very frail. On days when she was strong, she would get around her small government apartment using furniture for walking aides, but was awkwardly bent at the waist. This painful posturing gave the appearance of being nearly broken in two. On days when she was not as strong, she moved with the use of her wheeled walker. Navigation, on any day, was difficult.

She had nearly every major disease in the book: diabetes, hypertension, arthritis, heart failure, and others. She had very poor vision and gave up luxuries such as reading and any activity involving hand-eye coordination years ago. Mildred's heavy coke-bottle glasses rested heavily on her face, yet she lived independently and was happy. I never saw her in a bad mood or sad, and somehow she always made me feel better after our visits. I've always admired non-complainers. They are the ones who have every right in the world to complain, who have the most problems, but you would never know it by their demeanor. I hope to try that someday.

As many elderly people do, especially with visual difficulties, she was very patterned and scheduled, meaning she did the same thing, the same way, at the same time, every day. Surprises were not a good thing for Mildred, and that's how she managed to live so long without help. Other than an hour or two of assistance a week provided by the homemaker program and me, the rest of the day was her responsibility. Her being alone and so frail concerned me as this was before the life alert system, and more than once Mildred fell and had no way to summon help. I personally believe the life alert system is one of the best inventions of modern time. It's almost as if someone is with you round the clock.

On my very first visit I took an instant liking to her. Her smile was warm and sincere, and she had a beautiful, peaceful aura about her. Mildred had no family and was totally dependent upon the kindness of others to help her survive with some degree of independence. Could she have been safer, had better meals, and some much-needed socialization in a long term care facility? Most likely, but that's not where she wanted to be. She wanted to be home.

After I did my usual assessment, which included setting up her medication box that contained a massive amount of pills, I asked if there was anything else I could do for her before I left. She smiled her sweet, toothless smile, thanked me, and said that she didn't believe there was. With that, I told her how nice it was to meet her and that I would see her next week. As I turned at the door to say goodbye, I saw this beautiful little old lady sitting at her kitchen table unable to ever straighten or right herself. Her thick coke-bottle glasses were anchored snugly to her face with a rubber strap, and one hand rested securely on her constant companion, the walker. She smiled warmly again and waved goodbye.

Mildred had previously told me that every morning she made herself two eggs, toast, and coffee for breakfast. Again, this was part of her daily routine that was so necessary for her to be able to function and remain independent.

I made it as far as my car before I thought, Barb Tackitt, what is wrong with you? It would take Mildred at least thirty difficult minutes to do what I could easily get done in five. Get your lazy butt back in there and fix her breakfast. And so I did. I did the same every week for the next few years: two eggs over easy, toast with butter and jelly, and black coffee. How simple for me. How difficult for her. I was busy, but not that busy. She appreciated it so much and it surely gave my karma a boost for the day.

She would say, "Now remember, honey, don't have the skillet too hot or it makes the egg whites crunchy." This is another serendipitous lesson for me that has endured the test of time. Very seldom do I get crunchy egg whites, something of which I abhor.

What I Learned

I have seen literally hundreds and hundreds of patients in home care over my thirty-year tenure. Even though I tried hard to not have favorites, I did. There was always one constant presence in all of the patients that unintentionally found themselves wrapped around my heart. They were the ones with the most needs; those who could do the least for themselves. Ironically, the most dependent were not always the most appreciative, as I've some patients that I went above and beyond for, and they never so much as thanked me. But that's okay. I wasn't doing it for me. And conversely, I've had patients with just as many disabilities as Mildred but was far more fortunate to have more money, resources, and family, and they were just as appreciative.

There is just something special about being needed. Perhaps it's the middle child syndrome or the need to be needed, but I loved caring for those that I felt truly experi-

enced a positive change in their lives. "Mildred Day" was always a day of happy anticipation. She has been gone now for many years, but I hope wherever she is, she's being served two eggs over easy with toast and coffee on a silver platter.

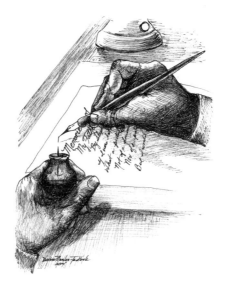

Stephen

Many people have a difficult time warming up to strangers, especially men. It is only after countless meetings and conversations that they begin to become comfortable. This was not Stephen. He was warm, genuine, and took an instant liking to people. I felt privileged just to be in his company.

At first glance, Stephen seemed quite ordinary, especially for a man born in 1903, over 110 years ago. The deep lines in his face revealed how he hard he labored in the sun's harsh rays. Winters were equally hard. His hands, from years of splitting firewood, operating a horse-drawn plow, and pumping drinking water from a well, were calloused and rough. There seemed to be nothing unusual or out of the ordinary about him.

But there was. Stephen loved to write; poetry in fact. He asked one day if I would care to read some of his work. Being intrigued, curious, and a lot skeptical, I said I would. What he brought to me was more than remarkable. Stephen had a large collection of unpublished poems that he had written over the years. But they weren't just poems; they were masterpieces. His talent and skill far exceeded anything that I had ever read. Most of his poems reflected on what was most important in his life; family, faith, hunting, and even a little romance. The following poem was written by him for his father and reflects the near-perfect image that I have of Stephen:

To Dads Memory
By Stephen Grove

If I were but an artist
What a picture I would paint
Not of a glorious sunset
Nor of a patriot saint.
But I would paint a picture
I can see the outline now,
Of a man with toil-bent shoulders
As he walks behind a plow.
I would paint his rugged features
Made so by sun and rain,
I'd paint the wrinkles in his face
Caused from times I caused him pain.
I would paint his bended fingers
Made so by endless toil
As he worked to make a living
For his children- from the soil.
Then I'd paint another picture
At the closing of the day,
As he sat upon his doorstep
And watched his children play.
But alas, I am no painter
But, Dear Lord, I ask and pray,
Let me keep this picture in my mind
On every Father's Day.

When I asked how a farm boy became a poet, he told quite a story. Stephen explained that when he was just a child, he had a cousin who lived too far away to commute or visit by horse and buggy. In order to keep in touch and remain close, they wrote often. But there was a twist. They only wrote in rhyme. This method of communication continued throughout most of his adult life.

Corresponding by mail was not an easy task in the early 1900s. The only modern writing tool was dip pen or nib that he continually had to dip into an ink reservoir or dip well. The convenient ballpoint pen wasn't conceived until many years later.

Stephen loved to talk, especially about his grandfather. Grandfather Grove marched with Sherman from Atlanta to the sea. "He also marched up the hill," he said, "to help clean up after Gettysburg." His grandfather said you could walk from the bottom of the hill to the top, if you wanted, and not step off a dead soldier. He was fighting in Brownsville, Texas when he was mustered out, or discharged from the military, and had to walk home. It took him six months to get back to Clay County, Illinois. His Mother didn't even know him when he returned, he had changed so much.

When Stephen knew I was honestly interested in his poems, he said he would see that I received a copy of them. Each one had been painfully and slowly typed on a manual typewriter. He knew not of today's modern technology with computers, copiers, and scanners. I feel another poem is appropriate here as it most assuredly reflects how many of our aging population feel: lost, alone, sad, just waiting.

Memories
By Stephen Grove

I wandered back among the hills
Where with my friends I played,
I sat beside the little stream
That wandered through the glade.
The birds that onetime sang so sweet
It seems they sing no more,
The swimming hole where once we swam
Was dry from shore to shore.
The sandbars where our bare feet tread
Have long since washed away,
And cattle feed upon the hills
Where once we used to play.
The stately trees that stood so tall
The axe have laid them low,
And in their place, like soldiers stand
The tall corn, row by row.
And those of whom I used to play
Most all have long since gone,
Have left me here to sit and wait
While they have traveled on.
For all of those that's gone away
I breathe a sigh of sorrow,
I only have to look afar
And wait for God's tomorrow.

What I Learned

One thing I have learned for certain; not all lessons are immediate. I liked his poems when he shared them with me nearly thirty years ago, but I didn't appreciate the value until I got a little older myself. Think of *how difficult everything was 100 years ago; the physical labor, writing by kerosene lamps, no modern technology, nothing of the world that I now live. Stephen's aunt had thirteen children but raised only four. Can you imagine? It's good to meet people like Stephen Grove to help put our lives in perspective. Maybe we don't have it as bad as we think we do.*

Tom

Sam lived in a very rural setting in Clay County. He was a bachelor and had lived alone his entire life. His rundown farmhouse was in disrepair, as well as his yard, farm machinery, barns, and everything connected to him. I'm sure it hadn't always been that way. Time and aging just has a way of making some things, like cosmetic improvements, less important. Some of his windows were boarded up or covered with plastic wrap. There was no grass in the yard, only junk cars, dead trees, and litter. His personal appearance pretty much mirrored his house and farm decor. His disheveled hair and unwashed overalls were more than in need of attention. But given that, Sam was a very personable fellow. I liked him. I would often take him homemade cookies when I made one of my nursing visits. The exact nature of my calls now escapes me, although I believe he had just been released from the hospital. My first responsibility was to be sure he had the basics: utilities, food, heat, and water. Then I would check to see if he had filled his prescriptions and that he was taking his medications correctly. I was also to teach him to live a healthier lifestyle, make better choices, and improve his overall health. Yeah, right.

Sam's yard was speckled with all sorts of animals. There were mangy dogs, cats, kittens, lots and lots of kittens, some pigs, and a few cows. Some of the animals were behind a fence, some were not. Those that were sequestered, like the cows and pigs, were not exactly secured by the fence but just too lazy to step over the sagging barbed wire.

Sam also had a turkey. This turkey was big, and he was mean. I'll call him Tom. Tom didn't like me, not one bit. Sam was too frail to help me battle this creature, so on my visits I was left scared and defenseless. It was solely up to me to defend myself against this hideous, feathered beast.

I recall one afternoon in particular. After pulling up to the old farmhouse, I felt relieved to make it in the house without much attention. Maybe Tom was preoccupied with something or someone else. The nursing visit with Sam went along as usual and with as much enthusiasm as I normally got. He really didn't care to change who he was or how he lived. After exchanging goodbyes, I headed for my car. That's when the "incident" occurred.

I stepped off Sam's porch and found Tom standing directly between my car and me. He was puffed up and had his wings spread wide to his sides. He stared at me as if to say, "Go ahead. Try to get to your car." I stood there for a couple of minutes as we engaged in a dead on stare. I slowly moved my body to the right. Tom, still puffed out with wings spread, slowly moved to the right. I slowly moved to the left. Tom moved to the left. The same thing happened if I moved front or back. He was on full attack mode. My car was close, so very close, yet so very far.

We stood there, just Tom and me, staring at each other without moving. I'm sure that we looked like Will Kane (Gary Cooper) and Frank Miller (Ian MacDonald) in High Noon. The

Marshall and the villain. The villain, wearing a black hat, was recently released from jail after being brought to justice by the white-hat-wearing Marshall. Each stand in the middle of the town, fifty feet apart, with their arms tense by their side. Fingers were held stiff and dangerously close to their six shooters. You could hear the town people whisper as tense moments passed while they waited for the first one to make a move. Soon it would all be over. Whoever won would be the fastest draw.

Or perhaps we looked like Father Merrin (Wm O'Malley) and Regan MacNeil (Linda Blair) in one of the last scenes in The Exorcist. Regan, clearly possessed by the devil (Tom) engages in a lengthy deadlock stare with the holy Father Merrin (me). This stare goes on for a couple painful minutes until Regan, desperately in need of being exorcised, finally and erroneously says to the Father, "This time you're going to lose."

Realizing the situation was not going to improve, I did just what Will Kane or Father Merrin would do. I went for it. I squared my shoulders, took a deep breath, and started running for my car. My shoes slipped as I rounded the back and headed for the passenger front door. Tom was right behind me moving furiously. As I got in and shut the door, I saw his poor, defeated body shrink and his wings fall to his side. I slid over to my seat, caught my breath, and settled in to drive away. Something in my competitive spirit made me roll the window down, now at a safe distance from Tom and say, "You didn't win this time, devil bird." As I drove away, I felt confident that the ol' turkey would think twice before taking on such a smart and worthy opponent as myself.

What I learned

There are many lessons that can be learned in life. For example:

- *When life gives you lemons, make lemonade.*
- *Don't sweat the small stuff.*
- *Stop and smell the roses.*
- *Whether you think you can or you can't, you are right.*
- *Count your blessings, not your worries.*
- *When you cease to dream, you cease to live.*

However, sometimes in life, just sometimes, there are no lessons. You simply have to take a deep breath and run like hell.

Epilogue

Over the years, I have had many patients that taught me things, too many to mention all of them in detail. I have been shot at, bitten, sworn at, thrown out, lied to, hated, judged, and loved. Instead of developing individual chapters for all of them, I decided to summarize the remainder of the more memorable ones into one chapter and bring you the highlights. Again, all stories are true. Any similarity in names is strictly coincidental.

• Just a few minutes prior to a home visit, one of our patients, annoyed with her homemaker, pulled out a gun and shot her. The patient only grazed her worker and the injury wasn't life threatening, but it was frightening all the same. Even though I was never truly afraid of the patient and never personally felt threatened, she was immediately discharged from our care and was never readmitted.

• Another one of our patients knew how to get quick results. She had a little, yappy Chihuahua that wouldn't stop barking even after many repeated attempts by the patient to quiet her. Growing tired of the barking canine, she made a plan and took action. She reached into her chair table, pulled out an air gun and shot the dog. They dog yelped, I think was unharmed, and retreated to the back of the house. The mere fact that someone would do that in front of someone else was a little shocking to say the least.

• Many times I have been given food as gifts. There is nothing wrong with that; we all have to eat and baking is something that many of my patients could still manage to do. A slightly unin-

133

tended, totally unaware, faux pas occurred when many of the cookies given to me were made with ants and roaches baked right in. I always accepted them, but declared that I had just eaten lunch and asked if it would be all right if I took them to my office to have them at my break. I learned very early on that the benefit of simply accepting the bug-infested cookies far outweighed the brutal honestly or refusal of them. The patients were excited, anticipated my visit and wanted to present me with something of which they were proud.

• Once I waited for a very long time in the driveway of a patient's house that lived far out in the country. While I was inside making my visit, the township oiled the road in front of the house and, wouldn't you know it, they ran out of chat (small, crushed gravel to cover the oil) before reaching theirs. So rather than wait until another truckload of chat to be delivered, I made the bad decision to leave. I slipped and slid all over that road until I finally hit chat. It took my husband hours and hours to remove the oil from our car.

• Once, while making small talk with a gentleman, I noticed that he had been going through a stack of mail. Most, if not all of the mail, was trying to sell something. Specials for roofing, 20% off windows, low financing on second mortgages, several catalogs, vinyl siding offers, and advertisements for deals. I said, "Don't you just hate junk mail?" and he replied very loudly and angrily, "This is NOT junk mail!" He was livid at the suggestion. I could tell he had no confidence in anyone who couldn't tell the difference in important mail and junk mail. He all but asked me never to come back.

- On more than one occasion, I encountered more than I bargained for. A few times I was asked to intervene on behalf of a patient who didn't necessarily want the help; the doctor simply knew they needed professional guidance. All cases involved infected, non-healing wounds or draining sores. After washing my hands and assembling my supplies, I pulled back the dirty, older bandage only to find maggots. No matter how many times that happened I never moved past the horror.

- Grace warned me to not pet the kittens, or half grown cats; they were feral, wild, and mean. I thought, You just watch, I'm a bit of a cat whisperer and will have these babies purring in no time. The kittens were so cute. I bent down to pet one and next thing I know the kitten had sunk her teeth into my left index finger so deep that I couldn't get her loose. I shook my hand forcefully and pulled at the kitten's mouth but it didn't budge. Once I finally broke loose from the Satan-like creature, I never tried that again. The following day I had to get antibiotics and a tetanus shot.

- One of my patients experienced the trauma of accidently running over and killing his wife in their driveway. They lived in a very remote area where there was no scheduled trash pick-up or ordinances governing or mandating you to mow your lawn or clean up fallen trees, overgrown brush, and weeds. Visibility navigating around in and around his long driveway was extremely minimal. Many people condemned him, and conversely, I can see how one might think this is an unthinkable and avoidable problem. But if you could see some of the deplorable, dilapidated conditions some of these people live in and have always live in, then you might not be so quick to judge. They are not mean or vengeful people. In fact, they are loving and faithful. They were simply not raised in an environment where landscaping and neat, manicured lawns was either plausible or necessary.

• While my husband and I were wealthy in many things, money wasn't one of them. You can imagine my "Queen of England" feeling one Christmas when he scraped together every spare dime he had and bought me a beautiful, knee length, black leather coat. At the moment it was everything I ever wanted tied up in one neat, pretty package. I wore it proudly to work shortly after Christmas and felt so special. During the day, the Health Department received a phone call asking us to check on an elderly man. The anonymous caller felt the gentleman was possibly being abused by his family. Our social worker and I went to investigate; me sporting my most prized possession. The gentleman in question lived in a small camper down in the river bottoms. When we arrived, there were at least three if not four generations living in the camper, they were all home, and they were not happy about us being there. The only heat was a dangerously dilapidated old wood stove; the smoke just rolled from it. The exchange of conversation grew loud, to the point of being threatening. I'll admit it, I was scared. I kept backing up as the grown men inched closer and closer and their voices grew louder and louder. Then, the unspeakable happened. What's that smell? Something was hot and burning. Sure enough, I had gotten too close to the wood stove. I turned around and a basketball-size hole had burned into the back of my coat! My beautiful coat. We quickly fled, and did make a referral to elder abuse that afternoon. As glad as I was to leave unharmed, my grief was for my coat. I'm sure I looked like a little girl burying her dead goldfish as I laid my beautiful, knee length, black, leather coat to rest.

- Repeated abuse of the elderly was, and is, rampant. I am speaking of all kinds of abuse: physical, emotional, financial, neglect, and sexual. The most common at 55% is neglect. Neglect is defined as a refusal or failure to fulfill part of a person's obligation or duties to an elderly person. In other words, just not taking care of Mom or Dad. Physical abuse is a distant second at 14% with financial exploitation finishing third at 12%. Little can be done about the incidence of abuse as long as the patient denies all accusations when questioned by authorities. A parent is a parent forever. In spite of bruising and emptied bank accounts, they will deny any involvement from a child. They "fell" or willingly gave the adult child all of their money, even if everyone involved knows it's a lie. The parent will simply not cause harm or press charges that may result in prison time for their child, abusing or not. The sad but sometimes true expression goes, "A mother can take care of twelve children, but twelve children can't take care of one mother." In suspect cases, I always continue to report it to Elder Abuse even if I feel the effort will be futile.

- Make no mistake about it, one of my least favorite tasks as a nurse is trimming toe nails. For a $10 fee, the Health Department nurses would go to your house, soak your feet, and trim your toenails. Ruth called one day and asked to be placed on our schedule. The next day, I went by her house and performed the usual procedure by soaking her feet in a pan of warm sudsy water and then trimming her nails. I left thinking everything was fine but received a fiery letter in the mail the next day. I hadn't "filed" her newly clipped toenails, and she felt slighted. If I'm not mistaken, she used words like "negligent" and "malpractice". I don't like it when people are unhappy with me. It bothers me a lot, so then next day I got the nicest card I could find, apologized for my lack of superior toenail cutting skills and sent her $10 back. A few days later I got a letter from her. Anxious to read her counter apology, I quickly opened the note, only to find the same $10 bill. Apparently some sins are unforgivable and I had committed the unpardonable. At this point, without feeling even slightest bit of remorse, I took the $10 and had a nice lunch.

A sharp, old-fashioned patient had a thing for correctness and always emphasized the need for me to spare myself a lot of grief and do things right the first time. She would say, "Barbara, if a job's worth doing, it's worth doing right, and if it's not right, it's wrong." Whenever my good and bad conscious would argue about cutting corners or slacking on a project, her words would creep into my mind and remind me to do it right the first time. Her advice has saved me a lot of grief and frustration over the years. So simple, yet for some reason, most of us want to do the exact opposite.

• More than anything, I learned that there are no perfect homes. In my naive adult years I often envied certain people. They were usually the ones who seemed to have it all; prestige, money, education, respect, successful children, and powerful positions within the community. I truly thought they were above the mundane problems encountered by the rest of us folks, but not true. I learned that no one skates through life without their share of hard knocks. Some are better than others at hiding and not airing their dirty laundry, but we all have skeletons in our closets. We all have problems. In fact, my personal message that is attached to all of my emails is simply this: Be kind to everyone you meet; for everyone is fighting a hard battle. You can't turn on a news report for more than sixty seconds without hearing of some stabbing, killing, abuse, poverty, or beating. We must all do our part to try and make the world a better place. If you have learned nothing else from me or this book, please never forget: Be kind to everyone. We are all fighting a hard battle.

Acknowledgements

I would like to acknowledge my dear friend and nursing colleague, Janelle (Jan) Nichols Phillips. We share a love of nursing that spans an incredible sixty-five years. We were both there; back in the day, when our patient's got bathed every morning and a back rub every night. We took a great deal of pride in our work and still cherish our memories. Jan is a 1950 graduate from Christian Welfare Hospital School of Nursing in East St. Louis. Her husband of sixty years, Doug, was proud of her nursing degree and often accompanied her while working for the American Heart Association. Thank you for your supportive words of encouragement along the way. They helped me to keep going on the book, even when my mind grew weary and it seemed to me that my stories would be of interest to no one. It has been quite a ride and I enjoyed every minute.